The Girl with the Secret Name

The Girl with the Secret Name

~

Yael Zoldan

First published in 2024 by Green Bean Books,
c/o Pen & Sword Books Ltd,
George House, Units 12 & 13, Beevor Street
Off Pontefract Road, Barnsley
South Yorkshire S71 1HN

www.greenbeanbooks.com

PJ Our Way edition: 978-1-80500-110-2
Green Bean Books edition: 978-1-80500-098-3

Library of Congress Cataloging-in Publication Data available

Typeset in 12/16 Garamond
by JCS Publishing Services Ltd, www.jcs-publishing.co.uk
Printed and bound by CPI Group (UK), Croydon, CR0 4YY

~

This book is dedicated with great love to my mother.
And also to my grandmothers and all the brave, wise
women who live lives of quiet courage and deep faith.
And to my daughters, both born and chosen,
who I pray will do the same.

~

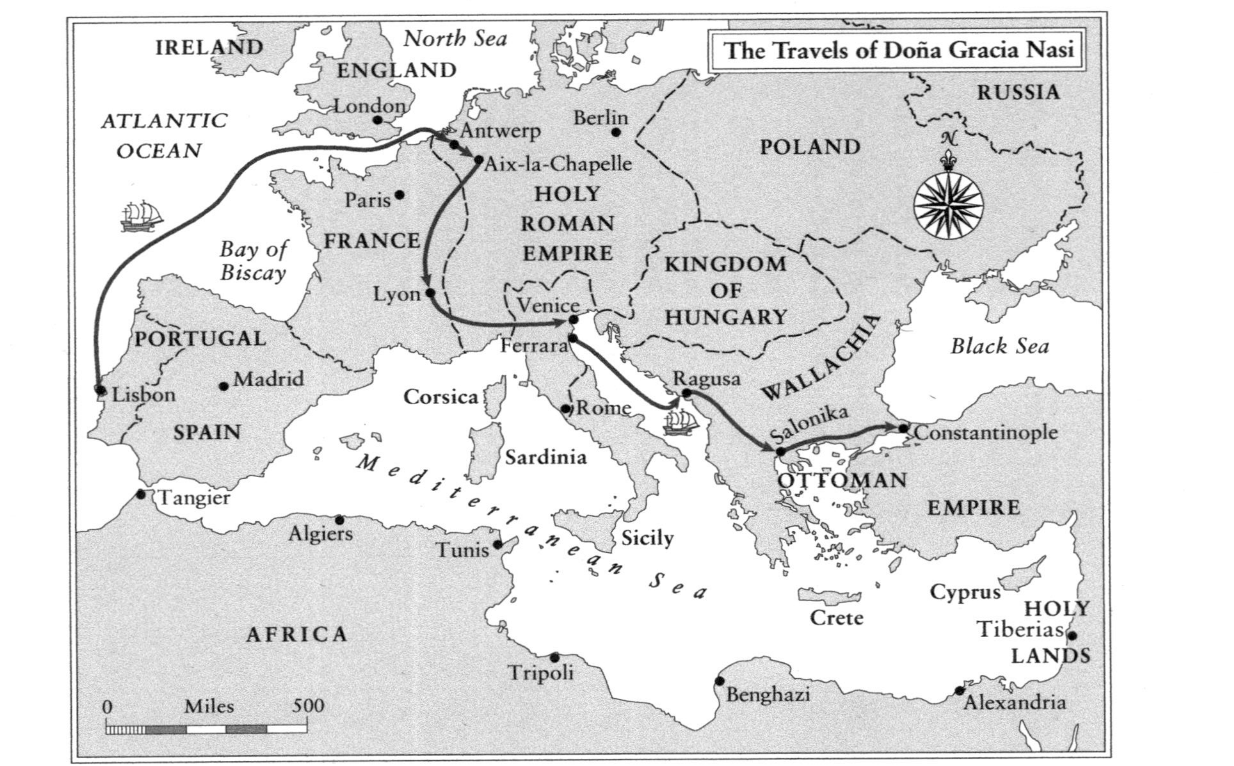
The Travels of Doña Gracia Nasi
IRELAND
ENGLAND
North Sea
London
ATLANTIC
OCEAN
Antwerp
Aix-la-Chapelle
Berlin
POLAND
RUSSIA
N
Paris
HOLY
ROMAN
EMPIRE
Bay of
Biscay
FRANCE
KINGDOM
OF
HUNGARY
Lyon
Venice
Ferrara
PORTUGAL
Madrid
Lisbon
SPAIN
WALLACHIA
Black Sea
Ragusa
Corsica
Rome
Salonika
Constantinople
Sardinia
OTTOMAN
EMPIRE
Mediterranean Sea
Tangier
Algiers
Tunis
Sicily
Cyprus
Crete
HOLY
LANDS
Tiberias
AFRICA
Tripoli
Benghazi
Alexandria
0
Miles
500

1

A Special Celebration

Lisbon, 1522

It was late at night in the town of Lisbon, Portugal. At the ocean's edge, sailors unloaded crates filled with spices by the silver light of the moon. In this same light, Beatriz de Luna sat at her dressing table, brushing out her long, dark hair. She had just bathed and her hair smelled faintly of the herbs from her bathwater. She looked at herself in the mirror and grinned.

Finally, finally, finally! Tomorrow was her birthday. She would be twelve! No longer a little girl. Tomorrow, she would wear the most fashionable gown. So what if the high lace collar was itchy? Mama had bought a shining, jeweled headdress for her hair. She would be glamorous and beautiful! Just last Sunday, in church, she had told all her friends about the plans for her party.

"Will there be custard tarts?" Christina asked.

"I don't know," Beatriz answered, "but we will surely have *pyramide de chocolate.* And we will have acrobats and jugglers to entertain us."

"Oh, I cannot wait!" breathed Alicia. "It has been so long since our last party. What does your gown look like?"

"I'll give you a hint: it's the color of the ocean at noon," Beatriz teased. "The rest you will have to wait and see for yourselves."

The girls chattered excitedly but Beatriz paused when the priest walked in, turning his nose up as he passed her. Why did it always seem that he disliked her? she wondered.

"Good morning, Father," she said politely, but he only stared at her with narrowed eyes. She was glad when he was at the front of the church and could not see her anymore.

Now, Beatriz looked at herself in the mirror again, turning her head this way and that. Did she look older, more mature? Did she look different now that she was about to be twelve?

"Good evening," she said, solemnly nodding at her reflection. The face in the mirror nodded back.

"Stop talking to yourself, Beatriz," her sister Brianda said. But Beatriz didn't bother answering. No one was going to ruin her good mood! Certainly not her sister, who was still only ten. What a child!

She flicked the back of her hand at Brianda and

paused to admire the beautiful gold link bracelet her grandmother had given her earlier that day.

"It's so lovely!" Beatriz had said, "My first birthday gift!"

"I carried this with me all the way from our family home in Spain and today I give it to you," her grandmother whispered and kissed Beatriz's cheek. "Because now you will be a link in the chain."

Whatever does that mean? Beatriz wondered, but she only smiled at her grandmother. "Thank you, Abuela!"

From the sound of deep breathing, Beatriz could tell that her sister had fallen asleep. She put down her brush and had just climbed into bed when her mother appeared at the door.

"Beatriz, are you asleep?" she asked.

"Not yet, Mama."

"Then come with me, please, child. There's something I'd like to show you in the cellar."

In the cellar? But there is nothing to see in the cellar! This must be another birthday surprise! Beatriz thought excitedly. With a great effort, she stopped herself from skipping as she followed her mother down the hall. She would be twelve tomorrow and must act like it even if it was hard.

But when she came into the small, dark room and saw her father standing there, staring at her with serious eyes, she suddenly felt afraid.

"Papa, why are you here?" she asked. "Is something wrong?"

"Hush, Beatriz," Mama murmured and pushed her gently into a chair. "Sit quietly and let your father speak."

Beatriz's eyes moved again to her papa's face and she felt a frightened, fluttery feeling in her stomach. Papa looked at the floor and cleared his throat.

"Beatriz," he said solemnly, "your mama and I love you very much. You have always been special to us. But, my daughter, you are much more special than you know."

"Thank you, Papa," Beatriz said, blushing, but her mother shushed her again.

"Just listen," she whispered.

"We, the De Luna family, are not what we seem," Papa continued. "We carry a solemn secret."

Beatriz couldn't help herself, "What kind of secret, Papa?" she breathed.

"We are guardians of a great treasure. We are links in a precious chain," Papa paused, and Beatriz felt her heart pounding. This sounded very exciting!

Her papa looked up and his dark eyes caught hers.

"My daughter, we are Jews."

2

A Double Life

Beatriz fell back in her chair, stunned. What was Papa saying? Of course they were not Jews! They were a Christian family living in a Christian country! Surely, this was some strange mistake.

"Jews, Papa?" she said, her voice rising. "But how could we possibly be Jews? We are good Christians. We go to church. We wear the crucifix. We are not Jews!"

Mama reached for Beatriz's hand and held it gently. "Yes, my darling. We do all these things, but we do them because we must. Because the Church demands it of us. Our bodies act like Christians but in our hearts and minds and souls, we are always, only Jews."

Beatriz felt as though the room were spinning. Tears came to her eyes. How could this be? Everything she had always thought was true, was not! She shook her head. Perhaps this was some strange dream? But it was not a dream. She could smell the meats roasting for tomorrow's party, she could feel her mother's hand on hers. This was real.

"No," she whispered. "No!"

Mama leaned close and looked deeply into her eyes. "Yes," she said simply.

Beatriz struggled to speak around the lump in her throat. "Then we will burn in Hell for all eternity," she cried.

"No, child!" Mama said. "Do not speak this way. These are only the lies they have told you because they fear you learning the truth. The Jewish people are a wise and noble nation, God's most precious children in His world!"

"Just as you are our precious child," Papa said, reaching for her hand.

"But then … then …" Beatriz pulled her hand back from his. "You have been lying to me all along! My own parents! If we are Jews why do we live as Christians? Why do you have us pretend to be what we are not?"

"Daughter," Papa said, "we never wanted to lie to you. We did it only to keep you safe. I know that this is hard to understand, but you must listen to me now. You know that our family came from Spain. In Spain we lived the truth. We kept the holy Sabbath. We worshipped the one true God. Then, thirty years ago, the king said that we must convert to Christianity or leave our homes. The Jews who were forced to convert were called *conversos*."

"So, that's when we became Christians?" Beatriz asked.

"No, child," her mother said. "We left. Our families were willing to leave our homes and our money behind to live as God wants us to. We came to Portugal. We started again."

"We came here before you were born," her father continued, "because we thought we could live here freely. But too soon the king of Portugal issued the same decree. He said that we must convert."

"Well, if your faith was so important, why didn't you just move again?" Beatriz asked, angrily. "Surely that would be better than lying all this time!"

Her father smiled sadly, "Because the king closed all the ports so we could not leave. He said that we must convert or die."

Beatriz tilted her head, confused, "But that is unfair!"

"Yes," her mama said. "It was a choice that was not a choice. So, we live this lie in order to stay alive. But always we hold tightly to our secret truth. They can force us to pretend, but they can never force us to believe!"

Beatriz's mind was swirling with confusion. Perhaps this was just a joke? Some terrible, nasty trick to make her believe something untrue and unkind. But she looked at her parents, sitting strained and silent before her. They would not play such a trick on her.

Then it was true! But how could that be? She slumped in her chair, her stomach a leaden, churning weight. Jews!! Who knew this shameful secret? Was her family in danger? Were there other secret Jews? Was anything what it had seemed before?

But when she opened her mouth to speak only one question came out.

"Why are you telling me this now?"

"Because tomorrow you will be twelve years old," her father said. "In Jewish law that makes you a Bat Mitzvah, a grown up. Now you are old enough to know about our heritage, the secret treasure we share."

"I do not want this heritage," Beatriz said bitterly.

"You do not want it yet," Mama said firmly, "but you will. There is so much about Judaism that you do not yet know, child. A long and rich tradition. Soon I will begin to teach you what it means to be a Jewish woman. I will teach you about Shabbat and keeping kosher. I will teach you the Hebrew prayers and you will want to learn more," her mother said.

"All I want is to be the same as everyone else!" Beatriz exclaimed.

"That is only your fear talking," Papa said gently. "It is understandable to be afraid of something new. But I have known you for all of your twelve years and you have never wanted to be like everyone else. You have always wanted to be special. And indeed, you are."

Beatriz's mind was moving rapidly, suddenly seeing things that she had never noticed before.

"This is why Abuela does not eat the meat of pigs! Not because the rich fattiness hurts her stomach," she said.

"Yes," Mama answered. "This is why, although we must never say so."

"And is this why the priest does not seem to like me?"

"Indeed," Papa answered. "He remembers our family from when we practiced Judaism openly and he hates us for it."

"Well, I do not much like him either!" Beatriz blurted.

For the first time since they had arrived in the cellar, Papa laughed.

"Well, I do not think it is very godly of him to be so nasty," Beatriz said, crossing her arms.

"It is not godliness that makes him behave so," Papa said. "It is hatred. And that is the opposite of godliness."

In Beatriz's mind hundreds—no thousands!—of thoughts were swirling, forming connections that she had never before understood. And all of these connections led to one great and terrible truth.

Her family were Jewish. She was a Jew. "But can we not choose to stop being Jews? Perhaps we can truly be Christians instead?" she asked, her voice trembling.

"Never," Papa said. "No matter how they threaten us, we will never let go of our heritage!"

"But why would we hold on so tightly, Papa?" Beatriz asked. "Even at the risk of our lives?"

Papa reached out and cupped her face in his hand, lifting her chin, "Because we are the Chosen People, Beatriz. We were picked by God to be His most precious children, His ambassadors in the world. This is a great and noble inheritance. It is worth any sacrifice to be the next link in the beautiful chain of our people."

Beatriz fingered her new golden bracelet. "I am a link in the chain," she whispered.

She looked up at her parents, a wetness coming to the corner of her eyes.

"Even if I do not want to be?" she asked.

"Even then," Mama answered, reaching to brush the tears away. "But I think that as you learn more you will want to be. Once we have cleared your mind of all the shame and lies, you will see for yourself how precious our heritage is. Come, child," Mama said gently and Beatriz let her head fall against Mama's shoulder. "I know how hard this is for you. And I am sorry," she squeezed Beatriz against her.

"Sometimes it can be painful to learn the truth," Papa said, "but it is a necessary pain. And you are a brave, strong girl."

But Beatriz did not feel like a brave, strong girl. She leaned toward her mother and fell into her arms, sobbing quietly. It felt as though her whole life was over. It felt as though she knew less than nothing at all.

After a time, her sobs ran out and Beatriz lifted her head and sniffed, wiping at her eyes. In the silence of the cellar, she understood that her life had changed forever. Now that she knew this secret, there was no way for her to escape it or even to avoid it. This was her new world, whether she liked it or not.

Her parents sat silently, worry and sadness in their eyes.

"If I must know this truth, then I might as well know it all," she said quietly. "Tell me everything."

Her father smiled, relief washing over his face.

"Oh, *querida*," he said. "There is so much to tell you, but the first thing you should know is that your name is not really Beatriz de Luna. It is Gracia Nasi. This is your Jewish name, the name of your soul."

"Gracia Nasi," Beatriz murmured.

"Yes, Gracia means favor, for we hope that you will find favor in God's eyes. And Nasi, our family name, means prince of our people."

"But we can only use that name among ourselves, in private," her mother warned. "And you must first make sure that no one is listening."

"Can I tell it to Brianda?" Gracia asked.

"No," Mama answered. "Not even your sister can know. When she is old enough we will tell this to her as well, but for now, she is still a child and cannot yet be trusted with this knowledge."

"Remember, Gracia," her Papa said, and a shiver ran up her spine as she heard the sound of her true name on his lips. "The punishment for secret Jews is death. Your life and the life of our family depends on your silence."

Gracia breathed deeply and squared her shoulders. Her world had shifted but she had not changed. She was the same person she had always been, even if she was forced to hide this truth from the world.

She looked at Papa and nodded fiercely.

"I understand," she said. "I will keep our secret. But one day, I will live freely as a Jew. And everyone will know my name."

3

Carrying the Secret

The morning of her birthday party, Gracia awoke with a start. She looked around the room she shared with Brianda. Everything looked the same, yet everything was different. Gracia fingered her new bracelet and looked over to the hook where her gown hung. It was hard to believe that her biggest worry just yesterday had been the scratchy lace of its collar. And today she was a hidden Jew? How could her world have changed so quickly?

Wafting up from the parlor were the smells of perfume, the sounds of cheerful chatter. Gracia hurried down to the yard, where tables were piled high with rich meats and nuts and musicians played lively tunes. Her brother Agostinho's children, Joseph and Samuel, were dressed in their finest clothing and she watched as they ran from table to table, grabbing candies and chocolates. Friends and neighbors streamed in, carrying beautifully wrapped gifts. And there stood Gracia, in the center of it all, smiling and accepting birthday wishes.

"Happy birthday, Beatriz!" Christina called, running up and kissing her on each cheek.

Surely, it is safe to tell Christina. Only her and no one else, Gracia thought. *I will take her aside and tell her everything. After all, she is my best friend!*

But before she could speak, Christina clasped her hands and said, "You look as lovely as Mary, the Holy Mother!"

Gracia froze. Christina's family were devout Christians, as were all of her friends. Did they hate Jews too? Did they hate her?

She looked up and saw Papa laughing as Mama straightened the lace cloth on the table. How had they kept this secret for so long?

In her mind, she heard Papa's words from last night. *Remember, the punishment for secret Jews is death.* She shivered. She had come so close to slipping.

"Come Christina, let's dance!" she called, gaily, spinning so her dress twirled around her ankles. But even as she laughed and smiled, sang and joked with her friends, Gracia was wondering. *Who are these people? And who am I?*

When the last guests finally left, Papa and Gracia stood at the door, waving goodbye. As Gracia turned to walk back into the house, Papa reached for her arm.

"Look at the doorpost, child," he said softly. "What do you see?"

Gracia looked at the large crucifix nailed into their doorpost.

"The cross," she answered.

"Look closer," Papa whispered.

Suddenly, Gracia noticed that under the crucifix was a narrow slit, almost covered by the nails. Had something hung there before? She looked up at Papa to ask the question, but he put his finger to his lips telling her to be silent.

"Out we go, birthday girl!" he called aloud and strode briskly out the door, pulling Gracia along beside him.

When they had gone a few yards down the lane, he spoke quietly.

"On the doorpost of a Jewish home hangs a mezuzah, a scroll with God's name to bless the house and its inhabitants. We covered the spot with the cross, to hide it. But things are not what they seem, Gracia. When you see the crucifix, think of the mezuzah. Think of our God and His love for you."

Gracia hesitated. "But, but … it does not seem that He loves us, Papa. In fact, everyone says that the Jews are heretics. That they are greedy, lazy, children of the devil." Her voice broke and she wiped away a tiny tear.

Papa squeezed her hand. "Is Señora Alvarez, the

seamstress, lazy, Gracia?" he asked gently. "Is kind old Señor Costa, the candy seller, a greedy man?"

He bent down to look in her eyes. "Am I a child of the devil? Are you?"

Gracia's mind whirled. Señora Alvarez was a Jew? Señor Costa too? And Papa! Kind, strong Papa. These were all good, caring people. They were not evil.

"Then why does the world hate us so, Papa?" she asked in a small voice.

"Because people hate what they do not understand," Papa said. "And they hate what they envy. The Jewish people have worked hard and achieved great financial success in many of the countries where we have lived. And more, we, the Jews, have always known that we are God's treasured children. Some people are jealous of our success and our bond with the Creator. And too often, envy becomes hate."

Gracia thought for a moment, "But children do not know about financial success, nor about God. So why would my friends care about this?"

Papa sighed, "Because hate is passed down from parent to child. And the children believe that the lies they hear are the truth."

Gracia stood quietly, thinking of all the things that she had believed to be true until now.

Papa put his hand on her shoulder, "We have taken your innocence, my child, and for that I am sorry. But we have given you something far greater. A heritage and a treasure. And for that I will never apologize."

~

The world had grown confusing. Each person Gracia passed, she considered. Were they secret Jews? Or were they Jew haters? Could they see that she was different? Would she ever feel safe?

One Friday, Mama called for her. "Tomorrow is Shabbat, the holy Sabbath of the Jews. On Friday night, our people light two candles. But I must not do that lest they suspect us."

"Then what will you do, Mama?"

"Watch me, child," Mama said.

Gracia looked on as Mama took an elegant candlestick from the closet and moved it to rest against a small mirror. Quickly, she lit the candle as she murmured to herself.

Gracia stared at the candle. In the reflection of the mirror, a second flame glowed. Her mother had lit one candle, but as she looked, she saw two!

Gracia leaned down, gazing at the flickering flames. She thought of how fire could bring warmth or destruction. She thought of how her new identity could do the same.

One evening, Gracia sat in the parlor with Abuela, practicing her stitches.

When the maid bustled out, Abuela leaned closely as though to kiss Gracia's cheek and whispered.

"From now on, as you go to church for the Mass you will remember. Their god is not our God. Their church is not our place of worship."

Abuela paused and looked around, "Whenever you enter the church and make the sign of the crucifix, you must think to yourself, "I enter this house against my will. I serve only the God of Israel."

Abuela cleared her throat as the maid returned to the room. She reached out and held up Gracia's cross work, "See this, child? If even one knot loosens, the whole thread will unravel. Pay close attention to what I teach you. Each stitch is more important than you know."

Gracia nodded her understanding.

She was a link. She was a stitch. She was more important than she knew.

~

As the weather grew colder and the wind howled at the door, Gracia spent more time with Abuela, learning the ancient knowledge along with her needlework. Outside the window, the trees bowed under the weight of the winter snow and Gracia huddled closer to the old woman. Her grandmother's gentle warmth felt like safety in a world that had grown dangerous.

When winter had passed, Mama called for Gracia to come down to the cellar to air out the spring linens.

As soon as the heavy cellar door was closed, Mama turned to her. "Tomorrow is the fast of Esther. We will not eat any food nor drink any water until nightfall to commemorate Esther's great sacrifice."

"But who was she, Mama?" Gracia asked.

"She was an orphan stolen from her family by an evil king. She lived in hiding, in secret, like us. Never revealing who she was. In the end, she saved her people and became a great Jewish hero," Mama said.

"A woman saved the Jews?" Gracia asked, astonished.

"Yes," Mama answered, "and we will fast tomorrow to honor her. We will pray that God remember us as He remembered Esther and save us once again."

The next day, Gracia did not take a sip of water, nor taste a morsel of food. All that day, as her stomach churned and growled, she thought of Esther. How terrible to think of that lonely young girl, taken from her family. Keeping her secret, all alone in the palace. Terrible, but wonderful too, for she had saved her people.

~

The months passed and Gracia felt that she was living two lives. All day long, she sat in school as the teacher spoke about the great Portuguese ships, sailing to India and beyond. As the nuns looked on, Gracia recited prayers she no longer believed. She learned the catechism and memorized the names of all the saints.

But it was at home that she was truly learning. Down in the cellar, Mama taught her the secret words she murmured to welcome the Sabbath. *Blessed are You, O God … Who has commanded us to kindle the Sabbath lights.* She told the story of Abraham, who defied the world to find the one true God. She spoke of Moses leading the newly freed Jewish slaves out of Egypt.

"There will be an end to our exile too," Mama said, firmly.

~

Time was passing as it always does and Gracia was growing up. She had become taller and more graceful. She felt herself to be wiser and sometimes a little sadder. At times she thought of the girl she had been on the night before she turned twelve and she missed that child. So innocent and full of fun! But other times, she was grateful for the richness of all she was learning. At fifteen, she was finally old enough to truly appreciate that she was chosen, special.

In wintertime, when night came early, Papa took her downstairs and showed her a page with Hebrew letters, folded tightly and hidden in a crack between the stones of the walls. From this page, he taught her the aleph bet. "These are the letters of the holy Torah," he said and kissed the page, reverently.

All around her, she discovered, there were other hidden Jews. Good people, smart people, kind people. People like her mama's cousins, the wealthy, charitable Mendes brothers and wise old Doctor Calvaro. Even the family priest, Father Geraldo, who came to their home on special occasions, was actually a hidden Jew.

"How can a priest be a Jew?" Gracia asked Papa when he told her.

"What better disguise than the priest's robe?" Papa laughed. "Watch him closely as he quotes from the Bible. Do you notice that he speaks with his face turned toward the east? He is praying in the direction of Jerusalem!"

Everywhere, it seemed, secrets were hiding in plain sight. Gracia watched and listened and learned.

And at night, she dreamed of Queen Esther.

4

A New Partnership

Lisbon, 1528

"We must prepare ourselves," Papa said, bustling in from the market. "I have heard rumors that the Inquisition will be coming to Portugal. And soon."

Brianda pursed her lips and turned away. Although Mama and Papa had revealed the secret to her when she turned twelve, she continued to act as though nothing had changed. Even in their room at night she would not speak to Gracia of it—as though by ignoring it she could make this truth go away.

Now, Mama turned to Papa. "Hush!" she said fiercely. "Don't speak of it and it will not be so!"

But it was spoken of everywhere. In school the girls chattered excitedly about the Inquisition.

"My brother says that the Grand Inquisitor spends his days and nights finding *conversos* who have only pretended to convert and he will not stop until all of Portugal is rid of them," said Christina, opening her eyes wide. She was seventeen now and took every opportunity to show off her dark, pretty lashes.

"It is true," Maria said, grinning. "He has special ways of torturing them and forcing them to admit their crimes."

"I heard that if they refuse to confess, they will be publicly burned at the stake! And we can all go watch," said Alicia.

Gracia nodded but inside she was shivering. She had always known that hatred existed, but what kind of world was it where even schoolgirls were excited by the death of Jews? And worse, what would they do if they knew she was one of them?

That afternoon, she and Brianda walked home quickly, their heads bent against the wind.

"Do you hear what they say about us?" Brianda whispered.

"I hear them," Gracia answered. "But they do not know of what they speak and we must be brave and strong."

"I do not think I can be as strong as you, Gracia," Brianda said, her voice quavering.

Gracia squeezed her hand. She must be brave for her sister, even if inside she was every bit as afraid.

At home she brought her fears to her father. "Papa," she said when she was sure they were alone, "all day, my friends speak of the Inquisition. They talk about torture and confessions and other terrible things! Tell me truly, are we safe here? Does the Church suspect us?"

Papa reached for her hand. "My daughter, we have done everything in our power to protect our secret, but people have long memories. They remember when we came here from Spain. That we were Jews forced to convert. No matter how careful we are, they doubt our sincerity and are always hoping to catch us out."

"Then we are not safe!" Gracia cried.

"Calm yourself, daughter," Papa answered. "As long as they cannot prove that we keep the old ways, we will be safe. They may not like us, but they cannot harm us."

Gracia thought of the priest's angry stare. He had known all along that her family were Jews and was always watching, hoping to see them slip. How could a man of faith be filled with so much hatred?

Later that week, Gracia sat with her abuela, embroidering handkerchiefs. Her voice was low as she bent close to the fabric.

"But how do we ever know who to trust, Abuela?"

"There are codes, *niña*," her grandmother answered. "Secret passwords that only we, the Chosen Ones, would know."

Gracia lifted her head, "But I don't know any passwords!"

"Shhh!!" said Abuela. "Lower your voice and listen.

If one of us says, 'They say it will rain tomorrow.' The other answers, 'The more it rains, the better my garden grows.' If the correct answer does not come, we know they cannot be trusted."

~

Late one evening, as Gracia sat sketching, her mother called for her.

Gracia followed her to the parlor and sat down. The last time her parents had summoned her, her life had changed completely. Was that about to happen again?

"You are eighteen now," her father began. "Eighteen in Hebrew is *chai*, which means life. It is time for you to start your new life."

Gracia's heartbeat quickened and her hands fidgeted in her lap. "My new life?"

"Yes, my daughter, the time has come for you to marry."

"Marry?" Gracia repeated, astonished. Why, only a moment ago, she had been drawing flowers. "But … but … to whom?"

"We have chosen well for you, darling," her mother said, smiling at Gracia's confusion. "Your groom will be my cousin, Francisco Mendes. With God's help you will be happy together."

Gracia's eyes opened wide. Everyone knew the

Mendes brothers. Her mother's cousins were fabulously wealthy and powerful men.

"Francisco Mendes?" she said slowly.

"Yes," Papa nodded.

"But … The House of Mendes is famous. They lend money to kings and noblemen. Even the pope has borrowed from their banks!"

"Yes," Papa said again. "And so?"

"And so … why would Francisco want to be married to me?"

Her parents laughed out loud.

"Because you are bright and good," Mama said. "And because you both share our Jewish heritage, which you will guard and protect in your new home."

"A Jewish home," Gracia whispered, beginning to imagine her new life.

"A *secret* Jewish home," her mother said firmly, the old worry in her eyes.

"Yes, of course, Mama."

And so began a beautiful courtship. Francisco was kind and charming. He took her on picnics and for walks along the riverbank. Sometimes he spoke of serious things, but often he made her laugh. Gracia felt light and happy when she was with him.

"Are you ready to be a wife, Beatriz?" Brianda teased.

"If Francisco is my husband, I am!" Gracia answered.

She turned to her sister. "One day, I hope you too will find a man like Francisco," she said.

"It sounds terribly boring," Brianda answered. "I'd far rather spend time with my friends."

Gracia smiled and waited at the window for Francisco to come for her.

That evening, as they walked, Francisco cleared his throat nervously, "Beatriz, I would like to bring you to Friday-night dinner with my family," he said.

Gracia's hand flew to her throat. She had seen the Mendes family many times at church and she knew that they were distant cousins to her mother. But they were very wealthy people, the most elite of their city. What would she wear? And, more important, would they be kind to her?

When Francisco came to fetch her that evening, her heart was beating quickly. But her fears were calmed as soon as she walked into the house.

"My new daughter!" Francisco's mother said, warmly reaching to embrace Gracia. "My heart is already filled with love for you!"

The servants brought out course after course, Gracia noticed that the garlicky, fragrant sausage was made of turkey and not pork. There was a richly embroidered tapestry on the wall, of a bird resting on the shoulder of a lion. She remembered her papa telling her that the bird symbolized the soaring hope of the Jews and the lion was for the kingship of David.

As the conversation flowed and their plates filled, Gracia looked at the corner of the room. There, resting against a mirror, was a lit candle. Gracia gazed at the two flickering flames and smiled.

~

When Gracia's friends heard about the engagement, they gathered around, twittering like a flock of birds.

"Francisco Mendes!" said Alicia. "You will be swimming in money."

"She will be swimming in spices," said Christina.

"In golden pools filled with silver coins!" said Dolores.

The girls all burst into laughter. Gracia laughed along.

"You may all come swim with me," she invited.

But inside, she remembered Francisco's words: "We will build our home on the foundation of our traditions, with goodness and with God."

There are riches these girls could never understand, she thought and smiled.

"Look at Beatriz smiling!" said Alicia. "She is dreaming of servants and jewels."

"You know me so well," said Gracia.

But they didn't really know her. Not at all.

~

In the darkness of the small, damp cellar, Gracia and Francisco stood. The four corners of the tallit above their heads were held by Gracia's brother Agostinho, Francisco's brother Diogo, and each of their fathers. Gracia's little nephews Joseph and Samuel stood solemnly holding a bottle of wine and a silver goblet. In the corner, Mama clasped Francisco's mother's hand in hers, their eyes shining.

Tears of joy streamed down Gracia's face as Francisco whispered the ancient words, "Behold you are betrothed to me with this ring, according to the law of Moses and Israel."

Gracia looked up as Papa spoke. "You are husband and wife now. May our God bless you and give you the strength to hold on to Him. May you bring pride to your people."

Francisco and Gracia each took a sip from a silver goblet. As the wine poured down her throat, joy filled Gracia's heart.

"Mazel tov!" Abuela whispered, the lines at her eyes crinkling with her smile.

"Mazel tov!" Gracia answered.

~

Sunlight streamed through the stained-glass windows on the morning of their Christian wedding. The bride and groom stood as the priest spoke on and on. Gracia pretended to listen. She looked out at the crowd. All the wealthiest merchants and most prominent members of the church were packed into the pews. From the front row, Brianda winked at her.

Finally, the priest stopped droning. "May the Lord bless this union always!"

"Congratulations!" the crowd cheered as the musicians burst into song.

Francisco leaned in and whispered, "All these people here to witness us marrying. And none of them know that we are already married!"

"That was our true wedding," Gracia whispered back. "This is just for show."

"Yes," Francisco answered, his voice low and grave. "But we had better put on a good show. Our lives depend upon it."

5

Secrets and Wealth

After the wedding, Gracia set about decorating and entertaining in her new home. Often Brianda came for tea, bringing fresh sweet rolls that Mama had packed, and the two sisters caught up with one another. At those times, Gracia felt proud to be the wise, older sister indulgently listening to Brianda's stories and gossip. In the evenings, Gracia enjoyed dinner with her new husband.

"What did you do today, Francisco?"

"Ah, some ships traveled one way and some traveled the other," he answered with a chuckle. "My work would bore you. Tell me about your day instead."

But for all of Francisco's insistence that his days were dull, Gracia found his business quite interesting. Over time, she noticed that there seemed to be two different types of business meetings.

Some men came each day to talk about ships and

loans. They walked through the front door, and Francisco spoke to them loudly and at length. But there was another group of men who came through the back door in the dark of night. With these men, the meetings were hurried and hushed.

One night, she brought tea to Francisco in his office. As she balanced the tray, she heard a voice inside the room say, "Six chickens must fly or be cooked."

When Gracia opened the door, she saw there was another man in the room, who quickly pulled his hood up to cover his face.

"Have I interrupted something?" Gracia asked, flustered.

"Nothing at all," Francisco said firmly. "And thank you for the tea. It will serve me well as I plan to work late tonight. Please do not wait up."

As Gracia walked up the stairs, she felt confused and a bit annoyed. Why had Francisco hurried her out that way? And whatever could "Six chickens must fly or be cooked" mean? Her husband was a banker, not a chicken farmer!

It was a week before her question was answered.

Gracia was sitting in the courtyard with her old schoolfriend Christina, enjoying a light lunch. Suddenly, Christina leaned in, her eyes shining as they always did when she had gossip to share.

"Did you hear the news from Spain?" she asked,

excitedly. "Yesterday, six Jews due to be burned at the stake mysteriously escaped their jail cells!"

Gracia looked at Christina and felt the small hairs on her neck rise.

Six chickens must fly or be cooked, she thought.

That night she knocked on the door of Francisco's office. He sat behind a wooden desk piled high with documents and ledgers. On the wall behind him were large maps, showing the routes of the ships of the House of Mendes.

"Gracia!" Francisco smiled. "I was just thinking of you. What brings you to my study?"

"Do you trust me, Francisco?" Gracia demanded.

"Whatever do you mean?" Francisco asked, confused. "You are my wife. I trust you with my very life."

"Then tell me. What does 'Six chickens must fly or be cooked' mean?"

Francisco sat up with a start. "Silence, Gracia! Do not speak of such things!"

"But if I do not speak of them how will I ever know?" Gracia asked.

Francisco looked at her intently. Then he stood up and went out to the maids' quarters.

"Tonight is your lucky night!" he boomed, jovially. "In honor of the festival of my patron saint, I give you all leave to go home. Hurry, hurry, while the night is still young!"

As the maids giggled and scurried out, Gracia waited. At last, Francisco returned.

"The house is empty," he said. "So you may speak your mind, Gracia."

"I am tired of organizing household matters and entertaining friends at lunch, Francisco," Gracia said. "I want to do something important."

"All the duties of a wife are important," Francisco answered. "You are the mainstay of our home."

"Yes, but what I really want is to join you in the business."

Francisco looked at her closely. "What interest have you in ships and oil and embargos?" he asked. "It would bore you to tears."

"Maybe so," Gracia answered, "but I don't believe that is all you do, Francisco."

She looked him in the eyes. "I am your wife. And I want to know the real work of the House of Mendes."

Francisco sighed deeply and rubbed his palm against his forehead. "Yes, you are my wife and it is my sacred duty to keep you safe. That is why I have never spoken of this to you. But now I will tell you the truth, and may God help us both."

He turned toward the maps on the wall behind him. "Look, Gracia," he said, pointing at small black marks on the map. "These ships travel to buy tea and silks and spices from Asia. And these other ships carry silver to the ports."

Gracia nodded.

"In cities across the world, we have agents working for the House of Mendes."

"Why do so many ships carry spices?" Gracia asked.

"Because they are needed for medicines and cooking and perfumes," said Francisco. "Did you know that pepper is worth twice as much as gold?"

"I did not," Gracia answered. "But from now on, I will be much more careful with my pepper!"

Francisco smiled. Then he grew serious. "There is more, *querida*," he said and leaned closer. "The loans that my brother Diogo and I make are enormously powerful. Those who borrow know that they owe us more than just money. They owe us favors. Because of this, they will do what we say."

"And what do you say?" Gracia asked.

"We say, we will lend you money if you free this *converso* from jail. Or we say, we will not make you pay if you resist the Inquisition."

Gracia stared at him, wide-eyed.

"Sometimes we say to a priest, if you need this loan, then help some of our friends. Sometimes we tell the king, there will be gold for your kingdom if you do not pass that law."

"You are using your business to help Jews," Gracia whispered.

"Exactly," Francisco nodded.

"And all this as you pretend that you are *not* Jews," Gracia said.

"Yes. It is a dangerous game we play. But we know that God is with us."

Gracia was silent for a moment, thinking of the six Jews who escaped and did not burn.

Then she said, "Let me join, Francisco. I also want to help stop the Inquisition!"

"In that case, you will be my partner," Francisco answered, "and we will do everything in our power to help our people." He looked at her gravely. "But we must do it very, very carefully."

From that day on, Gracia became an important part of the secret network of *conversos* working together to stop the Inquisition.

At the market, she approached a merchant selling baskets. "They say it will rain tomorrow," she remarked casually.

"Well, the more it rains the better my garden grows!" he answered, smiling.

Gracia leaned forward and slipped a secret message inside a basket.

"Enjoy your day, Doña!" the merchant called, tucking the envelope into his pocket.

Gracia smiled, knowing that the message would be passed on, along with a large bribe to a high-ranking official of the Church. *Just one more step to weaken the Inquisition*, she thought.

On Sunday, after church, Gracia chatted with Don Marco, the warden of the jail.

"The gossips say that there have been many arrests this weekend," she said.

"Yes, the cells are overflowing with *conversos*," he answered. "I do not have enough men to guard them all."

"Well, that must make your job so difficult," Gracia said, sympathetically. "But I have heard that some of those arrested are actually innocent of their crimes."

"Really?" Don Marco said, lifting his eyebrow.

"Indeed," answered Gracia. "Perhaps you might consider letting some of them go? It would certainly make your job much easier. And it would be a personal favor to me. Forever after, I would consider you my friend."

"A personal friend of Doña Beatriz of the House of Mendes," Don Marco mused.

"Yes. And I am very good to my friends," Gracia urged.

Marco nodded. "Tonight at midnight, I will open the cell doors. Then I shall step out for a short walk," he said, "and if some people were to disappear? Well, what can I do? Mistakes happen all the time."

Sometimes, Gracia and Francisco attended parties at

the Portuguese royal court, dressed in their finest clothes. The royals were happy to wine and dine them, hoping that the House of Mendes would continue lending them the money they needed to run their kingdoms.

"My husband, the king, is so worried about our debts," Queen Catherine sighed to Gracia. "If only there was a way to delay some of our payments to your family …"

"I understand," Gracia said sympathetically. "My husband worries too. The Inquisition is so dangerous and has grown so powerful. Innocent people are accused each day! If only our family had some sort of guarantee of safety from the king …" her voice trailed off.

"Well," Queen Catherine said, tapping her finger against her lip, "I know that for his close friends, even those with ah … more complicated histories, my husband sometimes issues guarantees that they will not be arrested."

"Oh, that would surely ease Francisco's mind," Gracia agreed, smiling sweetly. "He would be in such a good mood, I'm sure I could convince him that we don't need to be repaid just yet."

As the two women sipped their wine, Gracia thought of Esther holding her own in the palace of the king.

6

Joy and Pain

Lisbon 1536–1538

In this way, the years passed. Gracia and Francisco's home was full and busy with parties and social occasions. The House of Mendes sent ships to and fro, all while continuing its secret mission of saving Jews. But there are bad secrets and there are good secrets. And in the spring, Gracia discovered that she was carrying the most wonderful secret of all.

"God has blessed us, Francisco. We are going to have a child!"

Francisco's joy could not be contained. "A child to carry on our legacy. This is the most glorious news!"

And it was good to have good news at home, because the news from outside was very grim.

One evening, a letter arrived from Diogo.

"Portugal is getting dangerous," he wrote. "You must not stay and be caught in the trap of the Inquisition.

Join me, here in Antwerp. The branch of the House of Mendes that I have started here has prospered and we are safe from the bloodthirsty Church."

"Diogo is right, but it is not safe for you to travel now," said Francisco. "I will write to him and tell him that we will join him after the child is born."

The letter Diogo wrote back was filled with congratulations and good wishes for the health of both Gracia and the baby. "Stay a while if you must, but do not delay much longer, Francisco," he wrote. "I will be waiting anxiously to hear good news from you."

When their beautiful baby girl was born, Francisco and Gracia brought her to church surrounded by friends and family and had her baptized.

"What is her name?" demanded Gracia's young nephew, Joseph. "And can I hold her?"

Gracia looked at the handsome boy standing beside her and remembered him as a toddler, running in circles at her birthday party. She nestled the baby gently into his arms.

"We have named her Ana and I think she likes you," Gracia answered, smiling.

But when they got home, Gracia hurried to bathe the child and wash the waters of the baptism off of her tiny body.

"We will call you Ana, but your true name is Reyna,

which means queen," Gracia cooed. "Just like the brave Esther, you will be our secret Jewish queen."

~

And yet all the efforts of the House of Mendes, and all of the brave men and women of the resistance, could not stop the spreading poison of the Inquisition.

"Our worst fears have been realized, Gracia," Francisco said one evening. "The news has come that the Inquisition has been established in Portugal. All of our work has been for naught."

"Don't speak that way, Francisco," Gracia scolded. "We have done good work and we will do more good work. We must not despair! The situation may be more dangerous now, but nothing will stop our efforts on behalf of our people."

"You are right," Francisco answered, squaring his shoulders. "We will make plans to join Diogo in Antwerp and continue our good work there."

That night, as Francisco slept, Gracia sat up, thinking. *How easy it is to become discouraged, but I cannot. I must stay strong for my husband, my child and for my people. Even when it is hard. Even when it is very, very hard.*

On sunny days, when they walked together by the river, Gracia and Francisco imagined a better life.

"I wonder what it is like to live openly as a Jew," said Gracia.

"My parents told me that before the Inquisition our people were not afraid," Francisco answered. "On Shabbat, they lit candles and ate festive meals and sang songs about Jerusalem."

"Without fear, without hiding?" Gracia asked.

"Yes, *querida*," Francisco answered. "And one day, we will too."

"What a beautiful dream!" Gracia said.

But too quickly the dream turned into a nightmare. Francisco fell ill. Their nights were broken by the sound of his harsh coughing.

"You are strong, Francisco," Gracia said as she reached to smooth his blanket. "You will recover quickly."

"I am afraid that I will not, Gracia," Francisco said, struggling to catch his breath. "And if I were to die, you would have to continue our good work alone."

"Don't talk like that, Francisco!"

The thought of Francisco's death was an aching terror. Gracia could not imagine a life without him. As Francisco slept fitfully, Gracia sat by his side and pleaded with God to heal him. One day, Francisco reached into the drawer in his bedside table.

"I have written my will," he said, handing her a sealed envelope. "Do not open it until after my death."

Gracia took the envelope with shaking hands. The

thought of being without Francisco was too painful to bear. And Ana needed her papa! No! Francisco could not leave them all alone. She shuddered at the very thought.

Squaring her shoulders, Gracia hid the will at the back of a deep drawer and prayed that she would not touch it again for years.

~

But Francisco grew sicker. He was too weak to play with little Ana and soon could not lift himself out of bed. One terrible evening, the family doctor emerged from his bedroom with a grim look on his face.

"Doña," he said, his hands outstretched before him. "I'm so sorry to tell you …" He leaned down to whisper in her ear. "This exile is finally over for him. Francisco has gone to the God of our fathers."

"No!" Gracia whispered, backing away. "There must be some mistake!"

But there had been no mistake. Francisco was dead.

Gracia hurried into the room, closing the door behind her. Quickly she washed Francisco and turned his face to the wall, in accordance with the ancient mourning customs. She reached down to the bottom of her skirt and made a small tear in the fabric.

"I wish I could bury you with all the Jewish traditions, Francisco," she whispered, tears streaming from her eyes, "but I must protect Reyna from suspicion. May God have mercy on your soul, my husband, and shelter you in His arms."

The days passed in a blur of grief. A week later, Gracia sat in her black mourning clothes as Francisco's lawyer read his last will and testament.

"It seems that Don Francisco has divided his fortune," the lawyer announced. "Half of his wealth will go to his brother, Diogo Mendes in Antwerp. And the rest shall go to … his wife, Doña Beatriz and their daughter, Ana."

Gracia sat up straight. The rest of Francisco's great fortune to her and Ana? Why, that was millions and millions of *reals*!

At the age of twenty-eight, Gracia was quite suddenly one of the richest women in the world.

Back in her beautiful house, Gracia sat and cried. *I do not want these riches. I only want my husband back!*

Then she wiped her tears and lifted little Ana onto her lap. She stared into the child's small, sweet face and prayed.

"O God of Abraham, Isaac and Jacob, help me raise my child to be righteous. Let me teach her that in a dark world, she must be the light."

The little girl giggled and for the first time, Gracia smiled.

"Amen," she whispered.

Just then, she heard a loud knocking at the front door.

"Doña," her maid said, "I would not disturb you, but … it is a messenger from the king."

A chill ran up Gracia's spine. A message from the king often meant danger to a secret Jew. She hurried to the door and summoned the king's messenger inside.

"The king and queen are sorry for your loss," the messenger said. "It is a harsh world for a young woman alone with a child. But have no fear, the king will make sure that your daughter will be well cared for."

Gracia wrapped her arms around herself. "My daughter?"

"Yes," the messenger said. "Our lady, the queen, has kindly offered to take the child. She will raise Ana in her own household."

Gracia lowered her head, fighting to conceal the shock and horror that she felt.

"Please thank the queen for her kindness," Gracia said, her heart pounding in her throat, "but it has been a terribly difficult day and I must sleep now …"

The messenger nodded, "Of course. The queen will be happy to make arrangements tomorrow. I bid you good night."

After he left, Gracia went to Francisco's office. She sat down in a daze, feeling completely alone.

Why would the king take Ana from her? He certainly

didn't care about the child's welfare! Gracia kneaded her temples, thinking.

The king didn't want Ana. He only wanted her money. But … if Ana lived with him, he would control her inheritance. And he would control Gracia too. She would never be able to leave Portugal without her daughter!

The money is a curse, she thought.

But then she remembered all she had learned in her years with Francisco. She looked around at the maps and counting books.

Her eyes narrowed as she lifted her quill and began to write.

Your Holiness, she wrote to the pope. *Happily, I can pay you the 5,000 ducats my husband promised to you. In return, all I ask ...*

Diogo, she wrote to her brother-in-law. *I am going to find an excuse to bring Ana to Antwerp. My parents and yours are too old and weak to travel. But I beg you to make arrangements for my sister Brianda, and my two young nephews, Joseph and Samuel, to come immediately.*

She finished writing and took a deep breath. Then she went back to where Ana lay sleeping and brushed a finger against her warm cheek.

"Don't worry," she whispered. "I will never let them take you from me."

But despite herself, her voice shook. She was on her own against the king and queen of Portugal. She would need every bit of her wit and her skill in order to win this fight.

She stared down at her daughter and gathered her courage.

"It's all right, Ana," she whispered. "Where we are going, we will be safe. And safe is better than rich."

7

On Ships to Safety

Antwerp, 1539–1541

"Antwerp!" Gracia breathed, as she stared out at the busy, bustling port. She squeezed Ana's small hand as she recalled how the king had tried to snatch the child away. Luckily, the royal messenger believed her when she said that Ana was ill and could not be transferred to the palace. And thank heavens, they had gotten away in time!

Now, she looked up again and scanned the crowds, searching for Diogo.

"Look!" Brianda said, pointing at an elaborate carriage, flying the flag of the House of Mendes.

And sure enough, there was Diogo! He waved wildly and rushed through the crowd to meet them.

"Gracia!" he exclaimed. "Brianda! Welcome!" He knelt down, holding a candied citron in his outstretched palm.

"And you must be little Ana! I am your Uncle Diogo. We will be very good friends."

Coming up behind the sisters were their two nephews, Samuel and Joseph Nasi. The young men smiled shyly as Diogo drew them into warm hugs. After the weeks of travel at sea, it was a great relief to be standing on dry land, reunited with family.

"Thank heavens that you have all arrived safely!" Diogo said. "I only wish Francisco were here with us too."

Gracia wiped a tear from her eye. "As do I, Diogo."

"Yes, but at least we are together now. I hope we will make Francisco and our God in heaven proud."

"Diogo!" Gracia whispered fiercely. "Be careful speaking of God aloud!"

Her eyes searched the crowd, hoping that no one had overheard.

"Do not fear, Gracia. It's different here in Antwerp," Diogo leaned closer to whisper, "The law may forbid us from practicing Judaism, but no one bothers the *conversos* here. We are too important to the city." Then he stood up. "Enough of this serious talk. Let me show you to my home," he said more loudly, hoisting little Ana in the air. "Or rather, my home which will soon be our home, Brianda."

Brianda blushed. "I look forward to that, Diogo," she giggled.

Gracia smiled. She had announced that Brianda was engaged to marry Diogo only as a ploy to give them all a reason to escape Portugal. But it seemed that the two had taken a liking to each other! Perhaps they would be truly happy in their marriage together and the bond between the Mendes and Nasi families would grow even stronger.

~

It happened as she hoped, and after the wedding, Samuel and Joseph went off to school and Gracia and Ana, Brianda and Diogo all moved together into a large, beautiful compound.

"Look what a lovely house we have here, *chica*!" Gracia said.

"I see, Mama," Ana called, too busy running through the marble hallways to stop and listen.

Early every morning, Gracia brought Ana into the private woods behind the house. On the grassy floor she would sing the old Jewish songs to her daughter and draw letters with a stick.

"This is an aleph," she said pointing at the lines in the dirt.

"I know that one already, Mama!" five-year-old Ana said, impatiently. "Show me more letters!"

When their lessons were done, Gracia leaned against

a mossy tree, thinking of all that she had learned in the cellar so many years ago. As Ana skipped and sang, Gracia wondered, *What would Mama and Papa think of me now? And Abuela? I hope that I am making them proud.*

After a time, Gracia lifted herself up and reached for Ana's hand.

"Remember, it's a secret!" she warned the little girl. "A secret game that only you and Mama play."

Ana nodded and stomped her little feet in the dirt until all the marks were gone.

Gracia smiled down at her daughter. "You are more special than you know, my precious girl. You are a link in the chain."

"What chain, Mama?" Ana asked, seriously.

"The long and beautiful chain that connects our people all the way back to Moses, to Abraham. All the way back to God," Gracia said.

"I don't understand, Mama," Ana said, her little brow furrowed.

Gracia laughed. "Someday you will. But for now, remember we must keep this secret just between us."

Ana nodded. Even at her young age, she understood that some things were too dangerous to share.

~

On sunny weekends, the sisters walked and talked together in the courtyard. After a while, the joy in the house increased when Brianda gave birth to a daughter.

"We will name her Beatrice," Brianda said shyly. "After my wonderful sister."

Gracia reached to touch the baby's soft hair. "May she be a light to our people," she whispered softly. "May God keep her safe from all harm." She wiped a tear from her eyes. "But Beatrice is a very grown-up name for this sweet little one. She needs a nickname, I think."

"*La chica*," Brianda said. "Let's call her La Chica, 'the little one,' and we will never confuse the two of you!"

As Brianda settled into motherhood, Gracia and Diogo were hard at work. Each day brought news of the dangerous conditions of the Jews of Portugal.

"Diogo, the news from Portugal grows worse and worse. It is good that we have brought our own family to Antwerp, but how can we stand by idly while the rest of our Jewish brothers and sisters suffer?"

"We are not standing by, Gracia," Diogo said, leaning closer. "Let me explain ..."

That day, Diogo shared with Gracia the details of the House of Mendes' secret escape route.

"We set this all up when Francisco was still alive, may his memory be a blessing," Diogo said. "The *conversos* board our ships in Portugal, under cover of night and hide belowdecks with the spices. When the ships arrive in Antwerp, we send our agents to the docks to let them know that it's safe to come out."

"Oh, Diogo!" Gracia said, her eyes shining. "We must do even more. We must welcome them and give them hope for the future!"

And so it was. Ship after ship traveled the routes of the House of Mendes carrying spices, silk, currency … and hidden Jews.

At the docks, Diogo's most loyal agents boarded the ships.

"We've come to oversee the unpacking of the cargo," they called out as they went below deck to find the *conversos*, hidden between boxes and barrels.

"The crew is gone now," they whispered. "Follow us and we will take you to the home of the Mendes family. They will help you."

Whenever Gracia received word that the refugees would be arriving, she hurried to send the maids away from the house.

"There will be another crowd of impoverished people coming today," she said. "They are likely dirty and carrying diseases so you must stay away. Do outside jobs today and you may return when they have gone."

"And what about you, Señora?" one maid asked. "Are you not fearful of these dirty, homeless people?"

Gracia sighed. "I am indeed, and yet I must do my Christian duty and feed the poor."

The people who arrived were weary and frightened. Their clothing worn and tattered. *Had we stayed any longer, Ana and I might have been just like them*, Gracia thought.

When the refugees had gathered inside the house, Gracia spoke to them.

"My brothers and sisters, welcome to our home. Your journey has been long and hard, but you are safe now. Those of you who wish to stay here in Antwerp can work for us. For those who wish to journey on, our ships can take you to the Italian states. We will provide you all with funds to start out your new lives."

"Can we go to the Ottoman Empire, Señora?" asked one brave *converso*. "I have heard that Jews live freely there."

"It is true," Gracia answered. "The journey is treacherous, but we can help you find your way." She motioned to the platters of food that Ana had laid out on the table. "First you must eat and drink and regain your strength for your new lives."

"May God bless you, Señora," a woman called out. "You are as welcoming as our Mother Sara in her tent, as brave as Miriam in the desert. How can we ever thank you?"

"There is no need for thanks," Gracia said firmly. "We are family. And this is what one does for their family."

But though her house was full, Gracia was lonely. The weight of her secret, and all the things she could not say, made friendships difficult. How she missed Francisco and their conversations!

One night, Gracia sat down at her desk and opened a leather-bound journal. She smoothed down the page and gathered her thoughts.

If I cannot speak my hopes and dreams to a friend, she wrote, *at least I will confide in this diary. It is hard living this double life, although I know my work has value. While I wish I could share my heart with Brianda, I know that she does not care to know much about our mission. I hope that writing the words on these pages will give me the strength to carry on.*

She put down her pen and folded the diary carefully in a piece of linen, hiding it at the back of her drawer.

"Enough writing," she said aloud in the empty room, "there is work to do."

~

It was a bitter, windy day in the midst of the winter when Gracia called for the family's cook.

"Analisa," she said sadly, "You have worked here for many years, so I am deeply distressed to learn that you have been caught stealing our silver. Have we not always been good to you? If you needed something, you could have asked and I would gladly have helped you."

The cook looked up at her spitefully, "I don't need to ask the likes of you for anything. You will not fire me, no matter how much I take," she said, grinning nastily. "I know what you are, and I will tell."

Gracia raised one eyebrow archly and breathed deeply to keep her voice steady. "I am sure I have no idea what you mean by that, Analisa. Please gather your belongings. I am sorry but we must let you go immediately."

The cook left the room in a huff. "You'll be sorry!" she called over her shoulder as she slammed the door.

With her bag in hand, Analisa marched into the rectory, shouting for the priest. "They only eat special kinds of food, Father!" she announced. "And they slaughter their own meat. The Mendes family are hidden Jews!"

"I have long suspected them," the priest said, smiling grimly.

As soon as Analisa left, the priest hurried to the bishop's office, barely containing his excitement. "The cook accuses them, but there is more. Though Doña Beatriz comes to confession each week, she refuses to kneel and never actually confesses anything at all. Surely, that is proof of her heresy!"

The bishop nodded. "I will investigate the matter."

That very evening, spies of the Church descended upon the shipyards. "There's a reward for anyone willing to speak to us about the Mendes family," they announced. "We will pay well for any information we can use against them!"

"I have heard," a merchant said slyly, "that the refugees

who used to work for the Mendez family are now living openly as Jews in Venice. It makes me wonder whether the House of Mendes were hiding secret Jews all along. And why would they do that unless they themselves are Jews?"

"Excellent!" the official responded, handing the man a pouch of gold. Then he hurried back to the church with the new evidence.

~

King Charles received this information with great satisfaction. He and his sister, Queen Marie of the Netherlands, had been trying to steal the wealth of the House of Mendes for years. Now they had the evidence they needed to confront the Mendes family.

"What will we do, Diogo?" Gracia asked, when she heard what was happening. "We are in grave danger!"

"We will do what we have always done. We will use our loans and influence to run our operation for as long as we possibly can. And we will rely on God for His help."

"I am so grateful that you are my partner and brother, Diogo. I could not do this alone," Gracia said.

But she was going to have to.

8

A Woman Alone

Antwerp, 1542–1544

Diogo was growing older. He had lived so long under the threat of the Inquisition. Over the years, he had been arrested and falsely accused again and again, and many monarchs had tried to steal his money. The years of danger had taken a toll on his health.

In 1542, only five years after Gracia had arrived in Antwerp, Diogo grew sick and took to his bed.

"He is dying, Gracia," Brianda cried, wringing her hands together. "What will I do?"

Gracia looked at Brianda. *She has always needed a protector and does not have the strength to stand alone,* she thought. *I must help her through this and make sure she feels safe.*

"Be of good faith, Brianda," she said. "We will hire the best doctors to heal him. And I will always be here for you."

But despite their best efforts, Diogo continued to weaken and Gracia took to spending her time sitting at his bedside.

"Diogo, my brother," she said softly, "you have lived a life of bravery, and great generosity. You should find peace in the knowledge that you have been a credit to our people."

"I have always known I could depend on you, Gracia," Diogo said weakly. "Now, I would like to speak my last will and testament. Please call for my lawyer to write this down. I trust that you will follow each word, for I have made my choices very carefully."

"Of course," Gracia murmured.

When the lawyer arrived, Gracia propped Diogo up higher on his pillows, as the lawyer lifted his quill.

"I leave behind a great fortune and so I am giving clear instructions," Diogo said. "A sum of my monies must be given to help the poor and downtrodden. To my wife, Brianda, and my daughter, La Chica, I give all of my love eternally. The business of the House of Mendes, I bequeath to my sister-in-law, Beatriz. She alone will be in charge of our wealth, and she will be the guardian of my daughter."

Gracia's eyes widened in shock. "No, Diogo!" she said. "You must not do this to Brianda. You will die and I will be left behind with her anger."

Diogo looked sad. "It must be so, Gracia."

"Please," Gracia pleaded, "I do not want my sister's money. I only want her happiness."

"Gracia," Diogo said weakly, raising his head from the pillow, "we both love Brianda. But she is impulsive and fickle. There is too much at stake here and I fear that she will not use the money for the right things." He shook his head sadly. "It has to be you, Gracia. I'm sorry but it has to be you."

Gracia looked down at the links of her bracelet. She knew that Brianda was a weak link. The precious chain could not be broken.

"I will do it, Diogo," she whispered, burying her face in her hands.

As Diogo struggled to breathe his last breaths, the priest arrived at his bedside.

"I have come to give you the last rites, Señor," he said, holding out the crucifix.

But Diogo covered his face and refused to listen, choosing to die as a Jew.

~

After Diogo's death the family mourned deeply. But it was Brianda's behavior that was most worrisome. When she heard that she had not been named in Diogo's will, her fury ignited.

"I was his wife!" she shouted from her bedroom,

where she stayed all day. "I was his wife and I have been wronged!"

There was the sound of a crash as Brianda threw yet another item against the wall.

Each morning, Gracia attempted to go into the room and speak with her sister, but Brianda refused her entrance. Even La Chica was turned away as her mother thundered and raged.

Gracia held the little girl as she cried, kissing her forehead and smoothing her hair. "She is sad, my darling," she whispered. "She will grow calm again soon. I am sure of it."

When Ana came to draw La Chica down to play, Gracia reached for her quill.

I have lost Diogo, my partner and trusted friend. In secret, we washed him and dressed him according to the Jewish laws, so I know that we have done what we could for his soul. Still, the pain is terrible, Gracia wrote in her diary. *But I know that I must go on because so many depend upon me. Brianda is inconsolable. She will not cease her wailing, not even to take care of La Chica. She cannot understand why the money was not left to her and sometimes, God help me, I think that hurts her even more than Diogo's death.*

Gracia paused to dip her quill into ink. *My sister has always been like a lovely, spoiled child. Busy with her parties, never caring to know about our business and the great responsibility we have to our people. Diogo trusted me with La Chica's inheritance because he knew that I would not let Brianda squander it away on luxuries and foolishness. He only wanted the best for her, as do I. But how will I ever explain this to Brianda?*

In the wavering candlelight, Gracia caught sight of her reflection, saddened and afraid. She lifted her chin. *We will make our way, as we always have,* she wrote. *We will recover from this pain, and we will be a happy family again.*

~

While the Mendes family mourned, King Charles and Queen Marie rejoiced. This was the perfect opportunity to get their hands on the Mendes fortune.

"We can get to the money through the girl!" Queen Marie said, clapping her hands in delight. "Beatriz's daughter, Ana, is now fourteen years old. We will force her to marry our good friend, Don Francisco d'Aragon. Once they are married, he will control her inheritance. Then the money will be ours!"

"That is an excellent plan, Marie," King Charles responded. "With Diogo dead, there is no man managing their great fortune. Those weak women will not be able to resist us!"

That Sunday at church, rumors of the upcoming match between Ana and Don Francisco d'Aragon reached Gracia's ears.

"How exciting it must be for you, Doña, to know

that Ana will marry into nobility," the churchwomen tittered.

Gracia smiled tightly. "Yes, very exciting."

But inside she fumed. *My daughter will marry a Jewish man and build a Jewish home! No one will make us betray our heritage!*

The very next morning, a messenger from Queen Marie arrived at the house, inviting Gracia to a private meeting at the palace.

She is terribly eager to get my money, Gracia thought as she dressed in her finest clothes and straightened her spine. *Very well then, I shall meet with the queen, but I walk in with the knowledge that I am as noble as she. I am a daughter of the one true God, king of the heavens and earth.*

She looked at her reflection in the mirror. *I will be gracious because the future of the House of Mendes depends upon me. But I will not forget who I am. And I will not be cowed.*

"Doña Beatriz," Queen Marie purred, smiling sweetly. "How very fortunate you are! My brother, King Charles, and I have chosen to honor your family by arranging a marriage between your lovely daughter and our dear friend, Don Francisco d'Aragon!"

Gracia smiled with steel in her eyes, "How kind of you to think of her, Your Majesty! But my Ana is not yet ready for marriage. I thank the queen, but I must refuse this match."

Marie's mouth fell open in shock as Gracia curtseyed deeply, "Good day, Your Majesty."

Gracia strode out the door, her heart pounding in her chest. *I have angered the queen and I am in danger now*, she thought. *She is a powerful woman and used to having her way.*

She paused outside the palace and took deep breaths of the cold, clean air. *But I am a powerful woman too. And she will not have my daughter.*

After Gracia left the palace, Queen Marie paced the halls, fuming. "How dare that woman defy me?" she muttered angrily. "My treasury is empty, and I need that money. I will make Doña Beatriz agree, whether she likes it or not!"

"Alonso!" she called to her squire. "Wait at the docks and arrest every *converso* refugee who arrives in Antwerp. That will surely get Doña Beatriz's attention."

Day after day, arrests were made. Gracia clenched her jaw as she listened to the names of the prisoners being called out at church.

So, this is how Marie takes her vengeance, Gracia thought. Forty *conversos* had been arrested in the past nine days and many more were still in danger.

"Enough!" she whispered to herself. "I will not let her punish my people any longer."

Later that day, Gracia sat at her dressing-room

window, looking out at the garden. *What would Francisco do?* she thought. *What would Diogo advise?*

Suddenly, her head snapped up. "They would use our family to save our Jewish family," she said softly. "And I am not alone after all! For did I not bring my two nephews, Joseph and Samuel, to Antwerp along with me?"

She paused for a moment, thinking of the two brothers. Which one should she call upon now? Then the memory flashed into her mind of young Joseph's smiling face as he pleaded to hold baby Ana. What a charming boy he had been! And he was all grown up now …

She called for her groomsman to summon Joseph. When he arrived at the house, she ushered him into her office.

"Joseph, you are twenty years old now, and it is time for you to join the family business," she said.

Joseph sat up straighter. "Wonderful!" he said. "When shall I begin training?"

"Oh, you have been training for a while now," Gracia said, laughing lightly. "All those years ago, we sent you to school with members of the king's family in anticipation of this day."

"What do you mean, Aunt?" Joseph said, confused.

"You have become a good friend to the queen's son, Prince Maximilian, have you not?"

"Indeed, I have," Joseph answered.

"Well, now, you must use your friendship to gain an audience with the queen."

"And whatever should I say when I meet with her?" Joseph asked, puzzled.

"Joseph," Gracia said, leaning forward, "you are a bright young man. You do not know all the details, but I am sure you understand that our family has always used our wealth and influence on behalf of our Jewish brethren. Now, you must find a way to help our people. Flatter the queen with your charm and bribe her with our money, but get those Jews released."

Joseph's shoulders straightened and his chest seemed to broaden as he realized what was being asked of him.

"I understand, Aunt," he replied proudly. "It will be done."

~

That weekend, after a sumptuous dinner at the palace, Joseph asked Prince Maximilian for a brief moment with his mother, the queen. When the two were alone, he reached into the velvet bag at his belt.

"Your Highness," he said, holding up a magnificent pair of emerald earrings. "It is only fitting that a great beauty such as yours should be adorned by more beauty."

Marie's eyes narrowed with greed as she snatched them up.

"There is a necklace to match, but …" Joseph's voice trailed off.

"But what?" Marie demanded, entranced by the shining gems.

"But I have a small favor to ask," Joseph responded. "We could call it an exchange of sorts …"

Very shortly after, all forty of the *converso* prisoners were released and the emerald necklace was delivered to Marie in the palace.

Joseph's mission was accomplished, but the people all around the city were confused.

"Why didn't Doña Beatriz go and help the refugees herself?" the butler wondered. "Why did she send Joseph instead?"

"Perhaps she is unwell and cannot leave her house?" the gardener guessed.

"I don't think so," said the driver. "She has ordered the carriage prepared for a short trip tomorrow."

"Well, I know where she's going!" the local gossip whispered. "I heard that Ana and her cousin Joseph ran off to get married! Now, Doña Beatriz is going to drag her back!"

"That's not it!" another neighbor said. "Beatriz is so ill that she's near death. She is going to the hot springs in the south to improve her health."

The whispers swirling around the city reached Gracia and she chuckled.

"Why do you laugh when the town is spreading rumors about us?" Ana asked.

"Because that means that my plan is working!" Gracia answered as she hastily packed a few bags. "I myself started these rumors by whispering one lie to a servant, another at the market. I want the whole city confused so no one will guess why we are leaving Antwerp so quickly."

"And why are we leaving so quickly, Mama?" Ana asked.

"It isn't safe for us anymore, *querida.* The royals will not stop until they have taken our money and our freedom. We must leave before they come up with some other plan to harm us."

"But where will we go?" Ana asked.

"To the Italian states – to Venice. We must escape to find safety again."

9

A City of Islands

Venice, 1544

"I know we are all weary, but we are almost there," Gracia encouraged.

"Almost where?" Brianda asked, irritably.

It had been a long and stressful journey. For five months, Gracia, Brianda and the two girls had traveled in covered wagons, on dusty, unpaved roads. They had to stay constantly on guard from attack by the dangerous bandits who hid, waiting for travelers. Ahead of them was an unknown new city and behind them were angry monarchs who wanted revenge.

"We have been wandering so long. And for what?" Brianda complained. "At home, we had every comfort and all of that is gone now!"

"It is certainly hard to think of all that we have left behind. That is why we must look forward, to the future," Gracia said, forcing her voice to sound cheerful. "This is an adventure! And the tides will turn for us again. I just know it. But we must be strong."

"I can be brave like you, Mama," Ana said, loyally.

"I did not want an adventure," Brianda said bitterly, "and I am sick and tired of traveling."

Gracia breathed deeply, trying to summon her patience. She too was tired and worried. Still, it would do no good to let the children see her concern. They must believe that all would be well, that they would be well. And if Brianda could not do that for them, she would have to.

She turned to Ana and La Chica.

"Come, girls," she said, gaily. "Let us look out at the city. See how it sparkles in the light reflected off the water. So different from Antwerp!"

The city of Venice was built on a group of islands with waterways connecting one to the next. Between each island, the people traveled in gondolas, long, flat-bottomed boats. Dotted throughout the city were beautiful palaces with great windows and churches as ornate as jewelry boxes.

Gracia pointed to an especially small, crowded island known as the Ghetto Nuovo, separated from the rest of the city by an old bridge. Here, each of the narrow buildings was built seven or eight stories high.

"That is where the Jews of Venice live," she said.

"Why are those building so high, Aunt?" asked La Chica.

"The city allows Jews to live in Venice only if they stay in this one small area. But so many Jews came that there was no more space to spread out. So, they were forced to build upwards, into the sky," Gracia answered.

"Will we be living there, too?" Brianda asked in horror.

"No, I could not run our business from there. The Jews here are locked into the ghetto every night and forced to wear a yellow hat or scarf when they leave each morning. They are only permitted to work in certain trades. They do not yet have the freedom we hope for." Gracia sighed. "But within that ghetto, they are free to practice their faith. I envy them, in a way."

"Nonsense!" Brianda said, sniffing. "We cannot live caged up like animals. We are used to a much finer existence."

Gracia frowned. "That is true, Brianda, but still they do have something we do not. In any case, I have found us lodgings on the Grand Canal, while we figure out our next steps."

"Is the Inquisition here, too?" asked La Chica.

"Yes, my darling, and they surely know that we are *conversos*. But Venice is a city of merchants and the *conversos* are mostly left alone to conduct their business. The government here will not bother us unless we do something to make them gossip about us. So, we must do everything in our power to live quietly and not attract attention."

But Brianda was not interested in living quietly. She was not interested in that at all.

~

Slowly, the family became accustomed to their new city. There was a new language to be learned and a house to set up. Gracia and the girls took long walks in the cobbled streets of Venice. But while they hoped to settle peacefully into their new home, the royals of Antwerp were not ready to let them go so easily. Although Gracia had taken great care to slip quietly away from Antwerp, news of the family's departure didn't stay secret for long.

When the royals heard that the Mendes sisters had escaped, they were enraged. "Not only did they leave, they also took their money with them!" Queen Marie shrieked.

"Well, they won't get away with it!" Charles growled. Furious, he called for his scribe.

"Write this down!" he thundered. "I, Charles V, Imperial Emperor of the Holy Roman Empire, declare the Mendes sisters guilty of the crime of being secret Jews. In punishment for this crime, any property that they have left in Antwerp will be confiscated. All the debts owed to them will be paid to the Crown. Anyone found helping them will be severely punished!"

The beautiful house in Antwerp was raided by the king's men. All of the lovely furnishings, paintings and possessions that had been left behind were taken by Charles's men to add to his treasury.

The news reached Gracia in Venice and she sighed. She was thirty-five years old and it sometimes seemed that she had been running all her life. How long would she be harassed by greedy kings and princes?

Wearily, she sent a message to Joseph: "My nephew, you have worked hard to make connections among the royals to benefit our business. Now, I am sending you a great sum of money to bribe Charles. Please do what you can to save our fortune. We must be able to continue our mission of helping others."

When Joseph received the letter, he moved quickly to meet with King Charles.

"Your Highness," he began, bowing deeply, "I consider myself fortunate to know you and your family well. Many times, I have seen, with my own eyes, your keen sense of justice and compassion. And it is to this compassion that I appeal now. Perhaps His Majesty did not realize that the Mendes sisters were citizens of Portugal who only came to Antwerp to do business. Could the king find it in his generous heart to allow them to leave without punishment?"

"But what of their crime of being secret Jews?" asked King Charles.

"It is a falsehood!" Joseph exclaimed. "Even in Venice, they are living as good Christians."

King Charles folded his arms against his chest, unmoved by Joseph's plea for justice.

Joseph paused, "And to prove her admiration for the king, Doña Beatriz would like to gift you with 30,000 gold ducats."

"Indeed?" Charles said, opening his palms wide. "Why didn't you mention that before? I shall drop the criminal charges against them. But to truly prove the sisters' innocence, I would likely require even more convincing …"

Joseph looked into Charles' small, crafty eyes and nodded. "It will be done, Your Majesty," he said and hurried to send word to his aunt that more money would be needed.

"The loss of such a great sum of money is a terrible thing," Gracia said to Ana. "Our wealth is meant to be used to help our own people and not line the pockets of these selfish royals. But if this is the price of our freedom then it is money well spent. Joseph has done his best and I am grateful."

Once again, Gracia started over in Venice, reaching out to her contacts around the world to trade spices, grains and fabrics. "The House of Mendes has been re-established in Venice," she wrote. "You may have full confidence that our business will continue as always, and with fair trade, we shall all prosper."

Late at night, she climbed the stairs to Ana's room.

"Why must you work such long hours, Mama?" Ana asked, gazing at her mother's weary face with concern.

"The House of Mendes rests on my shoulders now, *querida*," Gracia answered, leaning to kiss her goodnight. "It is a heavy burden and a great responsibility. I must take care of our family's fortune so that we may help others."

While Gracia bore the family's burden, Brianda played.

"Prepare that delicious, breaded artichoke, and wine. Lots of wine!" Brianda called to the cook. "I will be having people over tonight for an evening of art and music."

"Brianda, we must be careful not to flaunt our wealth in this way," Gracia warned. "Remember, this place is just a stop on our way to safety."

"Oh, Gracia, must you always be so boring?" Brianda snapped. "Is it not enough that you have control of my money? Must you also try to control everything in my life?!"

She stomped up the stairs to her room, muttering as she went.

I cannot trust that we will always be safe in Venice, Gracia wrote in her diary late that night. *I must do what I can to safeguard our family's fortune. My eyes are always on the future, and I am taking steps to send some of our funds ahead to Istanbul, Turkey.*

Gracia cradled her head in her hands. Her shoulders were tight with worry and fatigue. Ever since Diogo's death, Brianda had grown spiteful and jealous. She could not forgive Gracia for owning the family fortune.

I love my sister and always will, Gracia thought, *I must continue to work to prove this to her. I will do everything in my power to make peace with Brianda and stay close to La Chica. Each day is a new opportunity for us to be loving sisters again.*

"Brianda, we rarely spend time together as we used to. Can we walk along the canal after dinner and talk as sisters do?" Gracia asked one evening.

"I have no time for walking tonight," Brianda answered, waving her hand. "My dear friend Isabella will be picking me up for a little party."

Gracia bit her lip.

"I'm glad that you enjoy Isabella's company," she said, "but remember, these people are not truly our friends. They do not know our secret. If they did—who knows what they might do?"

Brianda scowled, "They certainly are my friends even if they are not yours. Just because you are too busy to make time for pleasure does not mean that I must do the same."

Gracia looked at Brianda and wondered how two

sisters could be so very different. "Enjoy your evening, Brianda," she said quietly.

"I'm quite sure that I will!" Brianda responded, flouncing out of the room.

It will take time, Gracia thought, *but Brianda will eventually see that I have her best interests at heart. I only have to be patient with her, as I was when we were children. The love between us is deep and we will find a way.*

But Brianda was not a child anymore and all of Gracia's love and patience could not sway her. Anger and jealousy had hardened her heart and the distance between the two sisters grew.

Still, Gracia could never have dreamed that her own flesh and blood would betray her.

10

A Sister's Betrayal

Venice and Ferrara, 1545–1549

Brianda's rage grew and grew. Even as she danced at parties, bought new gowns and drank champagne, it festered and gnawed at her. At night, as she sat playing cards, her anger churned within her.

"Oh, I must go!" Brianda said, throwing down her cards, "I promised Beatriz that I would join her at dinner tonight."

"Why do you allow her to decide what you do? You are a grown woman," Isabella said, petting the fur pelt she wore at her collar.

"Indeed, I am," Brianda said, irritably. "And I am tired of being controlled by my sister."

On the rich brocade seat of her gondola, Brianda sat and stewed.

Why must we always be running from place to place? she thought. *I want to stay in Venice with my friends. If Gracia wants to wander so that she can practice Judaism, let her go herself. And good riddance to her!*

She fingered her diamond choker as she thought. But Gracia had control of the money, and without money how would she pay for her silken dresses, her elegant carriage, her jewels and parties?

Brianda's eyes narrowed. *I must find a way to get that money back. And I know just how to do it.*

"Go faster!" she shouted at the gondolier, eager to set her plan in motion.

The next day, Brianda spent extra time pinning jewels in her ears and arranging her gowns. She wanted to look just right for this important meeting. Then she called for her driver, "Roberto, take me to the courthouse!"

As they entered the courthouse, Brianda pushed open the doors of the inner chamber, her wide skirts barely making it through the entrance. "I have arrived!" she announced as she approached the justices.

"What business do you have with the court?" the chief justice asked, staring at the bejeweled woman who stood before him.

"Gentlemen, won't you help a good Christian woman?" Brianda whimpered, as she wiped a large, glistening tear from her eye. "I am in grave danger. My sister Beatriz Mendes is not what she seems – she is a secret Jew! She is trying to take my money from me and run away to Istanbul!"

The justices looked at each other with glittering eyes. It was all they could do to stop themselves from rubbing their hands in glee. This was exceptionally good news! For many years, they had been hoping to get their hands on Gracia's money, but they had no way to prove she was a secret Jew. And now this foolish woman—her own sister!—had marched right into their offices and given it to them!

"Judaizing is a very serious crime, Señora. If this accusation is true, we will be forced to take Doña Beatriz's money from her," they said.

"Yes of course, gentlemen," Brianda simpered. "You must take it away from her and give it to me."

"Well, we shall see about that," the men answered.

"Of course, I wouldn't use the money for myself," Brianda said, adjusting her diamond headpiece. "I only need it to care for my young daughter."

"Of course," the men said, smirking.

Brianda returned to her carriage, elated. The meeting had gone exactly as she had planned.

I will have my money back, she gloated. *The men of the court will take my side and I will have my revenge on Gracia!*

As soon as Brianda had gone, the justices cackled and congratulated one another on their good fortune.

"Let us write up a ruling," one man said, "stating that, because we suspect them of Judaizing, half of the Mendes family fortune must be placed in the public treasury of Venice until Brianda's daughter reaches the age of eighteen. Then we will be able to hold on to the Mendes money for years."

But Gracia had many connections around the city and she got news of Brianda's betrayal. She sat in her room with her arms wrapped tightly around herself, her heart broken with the knowledge of what her sister had done. And all for what? For money?

I would happily give this money away a thousand times if only I could have peace!

But there was no time to wallow in her sadness. Gracia straightened her shoulders and stood up, speaking aloud in the darkened room.

"I was not defeated by Portugal nor by Antwerp. And I will not be defeated by Venice."

Then she hurried to wake Ana, "We must leave again, *querida*," she said.

As the Venetian governors prepared to issue their decree, they could not contain their jubilation.

"Now, Doña Beatriz will never be able to leave Venice!" the governors crowed. "Because we will be holding on to her money!"

But they were wrong. Gracia was already gone.

~

It was not long before Gracia and Ana reached the nearby city-state of Ferrara. Here, Jews had always lived in safety and tranquility, protected from the Inquisition by the tolerance of Duke Ercole II. Like his father before him, Duke Ercole understood that the Jews were productive and intelligent citizens who brought wealth and culture to his city. He welcomed the community of *conversos*, who built fine homes, synagogues and businesses.

Upon Gracia's arrival, Duke Ercole II came out to greet her. "It is the great honor of my city that such a noble woman has come to live among us," he said, smiling. "You are welcome here and may live as you please, in accordance with the faith of your fathers."

"It is my honor to be welcomed by a leader such as yourself, Your Grace," Gracia said, curtsying.

Gracia and Ana walked beside the duke as he showed them the beautiful Palazzo Magnanini, a stunning palace with marble walls and gilded fountains, lush gardens and vineyards.

"I tried to find a place as beautiful as the women who would be living here. I hope you ladies will be comfortable in your new home."

Gracia smiled graciously. She knew that the duke understood that being generous to Gracia would bring him and his city great wealth.

It was not only the palace that made her smile. Here in Ferrara were many other important Jews, including famous rabbinic families, great poets and respected doctors.

As the prominent members of Ferrara arrived to welcome her, Gracia's heart warmed. All of these years, she had been isolated from other Jews, to protect her image as a good Christian. Now, finally, she could speak and socialize with others just like herself. But even now, as she lived in comfort, Gracia made sure to remember those less fortunate. She sent her servants to the town square to announce that she would be serving the poor in her courtyard.

"You will always have a place with me," she said to the orphans and penniless refugees she invited into her home. "We Jews are all one family. You will stay in my home, and I will help you find work here, in this fine city. And if you choose to travel further, I will assist you and fund your passage."

"Mama," Ana called one day, "have you read the poem that the great Spanish poet Samuel Usque wrote to the *conversos*? Listen!

> "Nor should you forget the help which you have had on the road from Portugal … the Lord has sent to you, the fortunate Jewess … She has been your strength in weakness, a bank where the weary rest … a fruit-laden, shady tree where the hungry eat and the desolate find rest."

"That is beautiful, Ana," Gracia said, smiling. "But I cannot be content with poems. We must keep doing more to help our people. Always, more."

Once again Gracia set to work building up the House of Mendes and communicating with her faithful agents around the world. Often, she stayed up, working late into the night, with Ana at her side for company.

One evening, Gracia looked up from her ledgers and put down her quill.

"Ana," she said. "I am forty years old now and have spent so many years hiding. Here in Ferrara, life is good for the Jews. We are not persecuted or threatened. We do not have to hide anymore. From now on, I would like to be known by my true name, Gracia Nasi."

"And I will be Reyna, as you and Papa named me so many years ago!"

"Wonderful, Reyna!" Gracia said, smiling. "And let us call for Joseph to join us too. There is work to be done and I can use the help of someone I trust."

"It would be good to be with Joseph again," Reyna said. "How I wish that La Chica could join us as well."

"As do I," Gracia said, nodding sadly. "But my sister is still so angry and has not yet calmed. Maybe soon, she will see that I only love her and want her with me, safe and happy. For now, we must go on without them."

When Joseph arrived in Ferrara, the small family celebrated. Gracia had come to depend on Joseph's good business sense and Reyna enjoyed her cousin's humor and charm.

"Joseph, I would like to set up a fund to provide aid to the *conversos* coming to Ferrara. And we must donate monies to the local charities, to build up synagogues and Jewish businesses!"

"Of course, Aunt," Joseph answered. "I have arranged meetings for you with the other Jewish leaders of Ferrara to plan and make decisions."

Gracia leaned back in her chair and breathed deeply. For the first time, she felt the comfort of working with other Jews like herself. She thought of herself in Portugal, dropping notes into baskets, and smiled. How far she had come from those days!

Still, she knew that there was much further to go. The Inquisition continued to terrorize Europe, and much of her own fortune was being held by the Venetian courts. She would need help to get that money back.

~

"I can never thank you enough for your generosity and kindness," Gracia said as she sat in the orange grove and passed the duke a sweet almond pastry.

"It is I who must thank you," he answered, patting his lips daintily. "The new hospital you founded will benefit all of my citizens! You are a very good friend to Ferrara."

"Then may I ask you a favor, as friends do?" Gracia asked.

"Of course," the duke answered. "There is nothing I would not do for you."

"Your Grace, surely you know of my legal troubles. It hurts my heart to tell it, but my sister, Brianda, has become confused. She has schemed to get the money that was legally left to me. My brother-in-law, Diogo, trusted that I would use that money to take care of her and their daughter and I have the documents to prove it." Gracia paused and drew a deep breath, "I am asking you to help me get back what is legally mine: the money and also the guardianship of my niece, La Chica."

"I shall do everything in my power to help you, my dear friend," Duke Ercole answered.

As she walked the duke to the door, Gracia was grateful but sad. How shameful to admit that her sister had plotted against her. How awful to have to ask for a stranger's help with Brianda!

When the duke arrived home, he called for his scribe.

"I have read Don Diogo's will, which clearly states that he held the highest opinion of Doña Beatriz," he wrote. "In her, he placed his hope and trust. And I too, can attest to the remarkable qualities of this good woman's character. She is known far and wide for her many virtues. By my decree, all of the wealth left by Don Diogo of the House of Mendes, will be returned to Doña

Gracia Mendes Nasi, along with all decisions regarding the raising of her young niece, Beatrice Mendes."

When Brianda heard what the duke had done, she stomped her feet in fury.

"I shall travel to Ferrara myself," she shouted, "and use the money of La Chica's inheritance to bribe the duke. I know that he will return it all to me!"

But Brianda did not arrive in Ferrara alone. A murderous plague came with her.

11

The Lady of Ferrara

Ferrara, 1549–1551

In the garden of the Palazzo Magnanini, Gracia was deep in thought. Beside her, Reyna sat embroidering. Life in Ferrara was peaceful. The Jewish community enjoyed respect and prosperity. They were poets and writers, doctors and bankers who met and mingled at their synagogues. Here the Jews did not hide.

The time has come to transmit our heritage to the world, Gracia mused. *Everything that once was hidden must now be revealed.*

She gathered her thoughts.

"Reyna, I have been thinking," she said. "Now that the family money has been restored to me, I would like to have Jewish books published. Books that *conversos* can read to help them connect with their Jewish souls again."

Reyna smiled, "Mama, if you have set your mind to publishing Jewish books then I am certain that Jewish books will soon be published!"

Gracia looked at her lovely daughter, busy with her needle and thread.

"Now, be careful with your crosswork, darling," she said, softly. "If even one knot loosens, the whole thread will unravel. Each stitch is more important than you know."

"Of course, Mama." Reyna nodded.

That very evening, Gracia called for a meeting with the scholars and printers of the community.

"We have been silenced for too long, my brothers," she said "The time has come for the words of our holy Torah to be spread throughout our nation. Words that even the most distant Jew can read, written in languages they can understand."

"Doña, we have the skill to print our Torah in many languages, but we do not have the funds," the printers explained.

"The money is not an issue," Gracia answered. "It will be my privilege to pay for the printing."

"Doña Gracia, you are the heart within the body of our nation," the printers answered, bowing their heads in respect. "You have always taken care of us, and we thank the good God for you!"

The Ferrara Bible was the first Bible ever translated into Spanish. As Gracia opened the front page, she smiled to see that the printers had dedicated it to, "The noble-hearted Doña Gracia Nasi, the Very Magnificent Lady."

At last, Gracia could breathe a sigh of relief. Her family was safe. The Jewish population flourished. The people of Ferrara were tolerant. It all seemed too good to be true.

And, in fact, it was.

~

In 1549, the Black Death broke out in Ferrara. The victims of this terrible plague were covered in painful blisters full of blood. Many of them died within days. And as quickly as the plague spread, the panic spread even faster.

For many years the Jews of Ferrara had enjoyed peace and friendship with their neighbors, but now the people were frightened. In their terror, they turned on their neighbors, blaming the Jews for the plague.

"Those foreigners have brought illness with them as they traveled here from Antwerp," the citizens of Ferrara wailed. "It is the Jews who are spreading sickness in our streets, just as they did elsewhere in Europe!"

"They must be exiled! They cannot be allowed to contaminate us good Christians!"

It was during this furor that Brianda and La Chica arrived in Ferrara laden with crates and crates of luxuries, embroidered cloth and golden vases, jewels, precious stones and books. They prepared to move to a rented residence so that Brianda could launch her next attack against Gracia.

As Brianda's many riches were being unloaded, the frightened people of Ferrara were gathering to protest to Duke Ercole, "Your Grace, you must quarantine them! Send these Jews to live in isolation before they spread the plague and kill us all!"

Duke Ercole looked out at the angry mob. He knew he would have no choice but to give in to their demands or he would have a rebellion on his hands. Quickly, he dispatched a messenger to speak to Doña Gracia.

"The duke sends his deepest apologies," the squire proclaimed. "As always, his friendship with the Lady of Ferrara is strong and deep, but he cannot ignore the will of his citizens. It is with sadness that His Grace informs you that he must expel the *converso* community from Ferrara until the plague has passed. But Doña," the squire said, bowing deeply, "the duke promises that he will always protect your household. The Lady and her family will be allowed to stay where they are. No one will harm you."

No one will harm me? Gracia thought, bitterly. *I am deeply harmed by the exile of my nation. Their pain is my pain. And yet I can say nothing to the duke except to thank him for protecting my household.*

The *conversos* were forced to leave their homes that very day. Strong men carried heavy cartons on their backs and women dragged bags along the dirt. Small children cried beside them. They did not understand why they should have to leave their homes. The elderly leaned on walking canes and plodded along the path. It was a terrible sight to see.

"I promise that I will do everything I can to help you get back to your homes," Gracia called out to the miserable people out on the road.

"Doña, you have always helped us and given us strength," the *conversos* answered. "No matter where we go, we will not forget your kindness!"

As the crowd trudged by, Gracia hid her face in her hands. "So many exiles we Jews have endured!" she murmured sadly. "How long must we wander?"

Tears fell down her cheeks, as she looked out at her brothers and sisters. The misery of the Jews continued and there was nothing she could do to stop it.

And this is why, she wrote in her diary late that night, *we must always keep our eyes on the future. There is nowhere in*

Europe where the Jews are truly safe, where they will not be blamed and sent away at a moment's notice.

It was in the midst of all this sadness and chaos that a knock came at Gracia's door.

Gracia opened the door to find Brianda and La Chica standing in front of her, piles of boxes and bags at their feet.

"Sister, I did not know you were in Ferrara!" Gracia said, astonished.

"Yes," Brianda answered, without a trace of shame, "we have only just arrived and the boorish soldiers of the duke have refused us entry into our own apartment. They keep talking about a plague. And what has that to do with me? In any case, we are in need of a place to stay. Since so many others dwell in your household, I am certain you would not be so cruel as to turn your own flesh and blood away."

How strange it would be to have Brianda in my home after all of our troubles, Gracia thought. *She has hurt me again and again. And yet … she is still my sister.*

Gracia put her hand out to Brianda and reached to embrace La Chica.

"Let me show you to your rooms," she said to Brianda. "You are welcome here with me."

Time passed and finally the terrible plague ended. The people emerged cautiously from their homes and began to resume their lives. As quickly as she could, Brianda packed her bags.

"I shall be leaving immediately," Brianda announced haughtily. "I did not come to Ferrara to be under my sister's control again!"

Sadly, Gracia watched Brianda leave. She had done her best to make things better, but her best had not been good enough. She kissed La Chica on the forehead and waved as the carriage drove away.

As soon as she arrived in her rented apartment, Brianda penned a letter to Duke Ercole.

"Words cannot express how terrible this time has been for me!" she wrote. "Living with my cruel sister was worse than dying of the plague! I did not have even a blanket on my bed or a bottle of ink with which to write a letter!"

As the duke read these words, he pursed his lips in disgust at Brianda's whining. He knew that Gracia had treated her well and that Brianda was only trying to gain his sympathy. Then he came to the next paragraph.

"Your Grace, I will pay you 40,000 gold ducats if you return my money to me. Gracia plans to take her wealth and move to the Ottoman Empire. But I promise that I will stay in Ferrara with my daughter, if you will only help me regain my wealth!"

The duke drummed his fingers against his desk. Surely, there must be some way to make this work to his advantage. But how? His friendship with Gracia was important to him, yet Brianda was promising a great sum of money. If only he could get Gracia to pay off Brianda, he would have the best of both worlds. He could continue his valuable friendship with Gracia and take the 40,000 ducats from Brianda as well!

"Scribe!" he called. "Pen a letter to Doña Gracia, immediately."

He cleared his throat.

"My dear friend, surely you must know the deep sadness of your poor sister, Brianda. She has approached me for my assistance in the matter of the return of her money. As I have always helped your people here in Ferrara, it is my fondest wish that you should help her today."

Gracia shoulders slumped as she read the duke's letter. The bitterness was almost too much for her to bear. *I welcomed Brianda into my home*, she thought. *I sheltered her when she needed me and yet she continues to attack me. And the duke, though he calls me his friend, knows that I cannot refuse him. Since he is so good to the Jews of Ferrara, I have no choice but to agree with him, lest he become angry and take out his revenge on my people.*

Gracia called for Joseph. "I am ready for this madness to end. Tell Brianda that I will give her 100,000 gold ducats, if she will only cease her war against me."

"Are you sure, Aunt?" Joseph asked. "That is a great sum of gold!"

"I am getting older, Joseph, and I only want to live in peace."

But peace was a distant dream. Danger was the reality.

12

In the Sultan's Land

Ferrara and Istanbul, 1552–1553

As winter neared, the days grew darker. Life for the Jews of Europe grew darker too.

"I have heard," Joseph said during dinner, "that in Portugal, the *converso* prisoners starve, chained to walls in shadowy dungeons. They are tortured until they confess to Judaizing."

"It is terrible," Gracia responded. "In Italy, too, the hatred for our people rises. The pope has ordered the burning of all Hebrew books. My sources tell me that guards break into Jewish homes and throw books into the alleyways. On the streets bonfires burn, incinerating the holy words."

"Thank heavens it is safe here in Ferrara," Reyna said.

"I wish that were true, Reyna," Joseph said. "But even in Ferrara, copies of the Talmud are being publicly burned!"

Reyna gasped. "What will we do, Mama?"

"We will leave before it is too late," Gracia said, firmly. "I have seen this Jew-hatred before, and I know too well how it ends. We must find our way to Istanbul."

"Will we be safe in Istanbul?" asked Reyna, anxiously.

"Indeed, we will," Gracia answered. "The sultan of Istanbul is a wise man. Not only does he accept Jews in his land, he protects their rights to live freely."

"Yes, but will the Italians allow us to leave?" Reyna asked.

"Never fear, darling," Gracia said, patting her hand. "I am working to find a way."

Later, Gracia sat, fingering her grandmother's bracelet. After a time, she reached forward and lifted her pen.

"Your Holiness," she wrote to the pope, "surely, you remember our friendship and the many loans of money and gifts that I have sent you throughout the years. Now, I beg you to grant me a letter of protection so that I may be allowed to travel safely. Without this, I might be harmed by evildoers on the dangerous roads and then I would no longer be able to help you."

When Pope Marcellus's response arrived, Gracia broke open the sealed letter quickly.

"My Dear Lady," the pope wrote, "with great pleasure I grant you this letter of protection to travel as you see fit, along with your family and whatever money you wish to bring with you. By my command, no one will harm you, no matter where you choose to travel. I value your friendship deeply, as I know you value mine."

Gracia breathed a sigh of relief.

"We have received protection from Rome," she said to Reyna, as she tucked the letter safely away in a drawer. "That is good. But it is not enough."

Her next letter went to her agents in Istanbul.

"Send word to Sultan Suleiman that I wish to come, along with my family, to Istanbul. I will bring with us our family's fortune and our many connections to benefit his beautiful land."

When the sultan heard Gracia's request, he laughed aloud.

"How foolish the monarchs of Europe are, that they persecute the Jews, their most valuable citizens," he said. "Good! Let their loss be our gain! Tell the lady that I welcome her. And anyone who harms her as she travels will incur my wrath!"

"Now we are protected by both Rome and Turkey. No one will dare attack us," Gracia said to Reyna. "We are almost ready."

Gracia's next stop was to see Brianda.

"Sister," she said, standing on the doorstep, "times have surely been hard between us. But life here in danger is even harder. I have attained permission for our family to travel to Istanbul, where we can live as Jews without fear."

"Istanbul?" Brianda retorted. "Why ever would I go to that distant place?"

"Surely, you must see that we Jews are not safe here any longer," Gracia said. "For the sake of La Chica, come with me while you still can."

"I would rather die as a Christian here in Ferrara," Brianda sneered, "than live as a Jew in Istanbul."

Brianda's refusal weighed heavily on Gracia's heart. She had promised Diogo that she would always protect his wife and daughter. She had sworn to keep them close to her! How could she leave them behind and travel half a world away?

"I have tried so hard to stay connected to Brianda," she cried to Joseph, "but she will not come and I cannot stay!"

"Leave in good conscience, Aunt," Joseph said. "You have done all that was in your power to do. Now it is time for the Jews of Istanbul to benefit from your great goodness. I will stay and continue to protect our interests here in Ferrara."

"I shall miss you, Joseph," Gracia said, wiping her eyes. "You are like a son to me. May God bless and protect you!"

The tears flowed like water as Reyna and La Chica parted. The two cousins were dear friends, as close as sisters. They both wept as they held each other tightly.

Then La Chica turned her tear-drenched face to Gracia, "Will I never see you again, Aunt?"

Gracia stifled a sob. "*Querida*, we share a name and we share a destiny. We will be together again. I swear it!"

As Reyna packed the last things into their bags, Gracia spoke with Joseph. "Inform the sultan that I will be arriving," she said. "Though my heart is full of sadness, I will not sneak into Turkey like a fugitive. I am tired of hiding. I will enter this new land with my head held high."

~

From the seat of her gilded chariot, Gracia lifted her gaze. The regal procession of forty horses and four chariots passed through sultry streets with glistening domes and slender minarets. The sultan had prepared a splendid parade for Gracia, to show his pleasure at her arrival and his even greater pleasure at the loan of 10,000 ducats she had already given him.

The places change and the royals change, but their love for my money stays the same, Gracia thought.

Lining the path were men in turbans, women wearing flowing robes and small children snacking on sweet halva. All had come to cheer the great lady's arrival.

And gladdest among them all were the Jews crowding together to catch a glimpse. "Doña Gracia!" they called. "Blessings upon you!"

"Who is that grand woman?" asked a young child, wide eyed.

"She is a princess of the Jews, come all the way from Europe," his mother answered, "a woman of great wealth and wisdom."

Gracia turned her face from the window and wiped a tear from the corner of her eye. "I am here, Francisco!" she whispered. "All those years ago, when I sat by your side learning the maps of the House of Mendes, and now I am here! Just as we dreamed … How I miss you!"

Straightening her shoulders, she took a deep breath, inhaling the cinnamon- and saffron-scented air. She pointed to the busy marketplace where merchants traded spices and silks, gold and precious stones.

"Do you see, Reyna, how the East meets the West in trade here?"

"I do, Mama," Reyna answered. "It is as though this is where the world comes together."

"And more than that, Reyna," Gracia said. "The Jews are prosperous here. They are artisans and bankers, translators and surgeons. In fact, the sultan's private physician is a Jew!"

"The sultan trusts a Jew with his own life?" Reyna asked.

"He does," Gracia replied, "and he is wise to do so. These Turkish Jews are learned, honorable and charitable. They take care of each other and live peacefully with their neighbors."

"How lucky we are to join this noble community," Reyna said.

"Indeed," Gracia answered. "In Ferrara, we lived safely but only at the duke's mercy. But here in Istanbul, it is our right to be who we truly are at last!"

When the grand procession was over, Reyna and Gracia moved into their magnificent new home. It was not long before the leaders of the Jewish community came to show their respect.

"We are fortunate to have you in our midst," said the chief rabbi of Istanbul, standing before her in his long linen robe.

"It is I who am fortunate," Gracia answered. "When I think that all of these years, we Jews of Europe have been hated and persecuted, exiled from place to place! And here you live in peace and prosperity."

"Yes, we have built a beautiful community but there is always more to be done," the rabbi responded.

"I would like to be involved," Gracia said. "I especially wish to help the refugees who come here find their way back to our faith. Let us work together to open new synagogues, build Jewish schools, print Jewish books, fund our hospitals. There is so much good we can do!"

"Much has been told of your great generosity, Doña," the rabbi said, smiling at her eagerness. "And I see that all of the praises are true."

Inside her own home, Gracia set up a large kitchen

and ordered her cooks to prepare generous quantities of food each day. "Let all who are hungry come here to eat," she said. "Announce it in the synagogues and in the gathering places. We have plenty and we wish to share it."

Each day, long lines of impoverished people stood at her door.

"Come, my brothers and sisters," she said to them, "eat and be refreshed, for you are welcome here."

"How fortunate we are that you are here," the people murmured. "You feed us like a mother feeds her children!"

Crowds of Jews streamed to Gracia's house to ask her for advice, for loans, for help in every way.

"Are you not tired out by the needs of all of these people, Mama?" Reyna asked.

"This work does not tire me. It gives me strength!" Gracia said, her face shining. "For too many years my people have suffered. It is my joy to finally help them without hiding."

And to add to their joy, in the spring, a letter arrived saying that Joseph would soon be joining them in Istanbul.

"What wonderful news!" Reyna cried. "I have missed him so!"

On the day of Joseph's arrival, Gracia laid out a beautiful banquet to celebrate. When Joseph's carriage pulled up in front of the house, Reyna rushed out to greet him.

"How good it is to see you, Joseph!" she exclaimed.

"I am even happier to see you," he said, smiling.

Turning to face Gracia, he dropped his bags on the shining marble floors. With a nervous glance at Reyna, he turned to face Gracia.

"Aunt, I have always felt like a son to you. And now, I would like to truly be your son." He paused. "I would like to ask for your permission … to marry Reyna."

Reyna's eyes shone with hope as she turned to her mother. "Oh, Mama, please say yes!"

Gracia clasped her hands together joyfully, "Nothing would give me greater happiness!"

But as joy and celebration warmed Gracia's heart, a terrible fire was being kindled in Rome.

13

The Fire Burns

Rome, 1556

In the luxurious inner chambers of the Vatican, the newly elected pope, Paul IV, raged. *Here I sit*, he thought, *finally, chosen as the most powerful man in the Christian world and still there are Jews living, doing business, prospering in my country.*

Pope Paul IV hated many things but what he hated the most was Jews. All of his life, he had learned that the Jews were vermin. Dirty, rotten creatures filled with greed, who refused to believe in the Christian god. All of his life, he had waited to reach this position of power so he could be the one who eliminated these vile beings from his land.

"The food is bitter in my mouth," he said, shoving away his platter full of sumptuous meats. "The wine tastes like sour vinegar. Nothing pleases me, nor will anything ever please me, as long as the Jews live freely in Rome."

"Have you considered trying the chicken instead, Your Eminence?" his manservant said meekly.

"I said NOTHING!" the pope roared, as his servant scuttered away.

"If I cannot rid this country of Jews," he seethed, "then I shall make life more and more difficult for them. Have the scribe write down my decree, 'From this day forth, each city may have only one synagogue.'"

"But, Your Holiness, in Rome alone, there are seven synagogues," his bishops said.

"Not anymore!" the pope thundered. "Close down all but one."

"Yes, Your Holiness," they answered, cowed by his rage.

"And why do these brazen Jews continue to walk around freely in the holy city of Rome? I do not care if they are *conversos* or not," he said. "These streets are made for good Christians, let the Jews live within a ghetto among their own kind."

"Yes, Your Holiness," they answered.

Within weeks, the pope's soldiers were out in the streets of Rome, chasing Jews out of their houses and into the newly constructed ghetto.

"How can you force us to leave?" the astonished merchants asked. "These are our homes which we have bought and paid for!"

But the armies of the pope chased them, brandishing swords and shouting, "Out, Jews! Out!"

As the children wailed and old women wept, the pope watched from his balcony, waving his fist in the air.

"Faster! Faster!" he shouted to the guards herding the terrified Jews into the crowded ghetto.

"I have had yet another wonderful idea," the pope announced the following week. "On the days of the Christian feasts, I want the Jews to compete in games for us to watch."

"What kind of games?" the bishops asked.

"It would be most amusing if they were made to crawl with ropes tied around their necks. Then they could be ridden like horses by our soldiers," the pope said, smiling.

"As you wish, Your Eminence," the bishops responded.

Inside the ghetto the Jews suffered terribly. They, who had lived in beautiful homes, now quickly fell into poverty. The ghetto was overcrowded, filled with rats and roaches. Quickly, diseases spread, taking the lives of the young and the elderly.

"Woe on us," the Jews cried to one another. "How long must we be hated and persecuted?"

The wails of the *conversos* reached the pope in his chambers and they were like music to his ears. The more miserable it was for the Jews, the happier the pope grew.

~

"Are you pleased now, Your Eminence?" the bishops asked when the ghetto gates clanged shut one evening.

"Pleased?" thundered Pope Paul. "How could I possibly be pleased when in the nearby city of Ancona Jews live freely and happily?"

He leaned down from his chair and bellowed a hot breath of air at the gathered bishops. "I am greatly displeased!"

"Apologies, Your Eminence," the bishops whispered.

The pope banged his fist against the burnished wood of his desk.

"The possessions of all the *conversos* of Ancona must be confiscated and given to the Church. And when that is done, arrest them on the charge of Judaizing!"

"But, Your Holiness, there are many known *conversos* in Ancona," one bishop said meekly. "It will not be simple to arrest them all. There will be an outcry among all the merchants. Even the Christian merchants will be hurt as their business is disrupted."

Pope Paul brought his furious face close to the bishop's.

"Do you dare question me?" he hissed, spittle flying into the other man's eyes. "Do you argue with the Holy Father, leader of the Christian Church?"

"No, Your Holiness," the bishop whispered. "It will be done."

Without delay, the army of the Inquisition swooped

down on the *conversos* of Ancona, arresting entire families. The guards shoved and pushed them into their prison cells, slamming the cell doors behind them as babies cried and huddled against their mothers.

"Now, force them to confess their crimes!" Pope Paul said, sneering. "Whoever does not confess will be burned in the *auto da fé*!"

The guards hurried to fulfill the pope's decree, swooping down on the frightened prisoners one by one.

"You will languish in this prison until you admit your sins!" they shouted.

"Signor," a man responded, "we have done nothing wrong!"

"Liar! You are accused of putting your hands on the heads of your children and not blessing them with the sign of the cross!"

"I have done nothing wrong!" the prisoner moaned. "Please just let me go back to my home."

"You are charged with lighting the candles on Friday night," they accused a frightened young mother.

"It is a falsehood!" she exclaimed.

"You will stay here in this cell without a morsel of food until you confess!" they shouted.

The next prisoner was dragged out, "You are accused of eating unleavened bread on Passover!"

"No, Signor!" the old woman begged. "Have mercy on an old lady!"

"Of refusing to eat food on the fast of Yom Kippur!" they shouted at a child.

They yanked a prosperous merchant out of his cell and pushed him against the wall. "You were observed sitting on a low chair when your mother died."

In every cell they accused and threatened the prisoners, young and old, without mercy. "Judaizers, confess!"

"I did not do it! I am a good Christian," an old man cried. "Please set us free."

But as long as the *conversos* denied, the accusations continued. Until finally, many confessed in the hope of being released.

"Please!" they sobbed to the guards. "We have confessed to our sins, and we will do our penance. Do you not remember that we are good citizens, your neighbors, and friends? If you are men of God, then please let us go!"

Through the bars of their cells, the bewildered, terrified Jews called out to their former neighbors.

"Friends, have we not always been good, upstanding citizens of Ancona? Help us! Surely you must remember the many times that we have acted in kindness for you and for your families. Please save us! And, if you will not do it for our sakes, at least do it for our innocent children!"

But the Inquisitors were not softened by their pleas. And the people of Ancona made no move to help them.

~

When news reached Gracia of what was happening in Ancona, she trembled in fury.

"My people have suffered enough. I will beseech Sultan Suleiman to help me stop this pope from his evil deeds."

The sultan sat on a jewel-studded throne in a room of silver and gold that sparkled in the sun streaming through the high windows. All around him stood advisors wearing long caftans and turbans of white silk and guards brandishing spears.

"The noble lady, Doña Gracia, is here to petition a favor from Sultan Suleiman, the Magnificent, Commander of the Faithful, Shadow of God, Lord of the Lords of the World!" a courtier announced.

Gracia stood with her hands at her sides, gathering her courage to face the grand leader of the Ottoman Empire.

"Oh, Magnificent and Honorable Majesty, I come before you in humility, to plead my case. Surely, in your great wisdom, you have heard of the plight of the Jews of Ancona," Gracia said, her head bowed to show her respect. "I ask for the sultan's help to have these merchants released. Without them, I cannot continue my business."

Gracia peeked slyly up at the sultan, fixing her gaze on his ermine trimmed cape, "The business I use to make the money with which I gift my good friend, the Sultan," she said.

"This affects your business, does it? Well, then I understand the problem very well, my lady," the sultan answered. "And I, Suleiman the Magnificent, am deeply moved by the trouble of your people."

He thought for a moment, "In fact, is it not possible that some of those arrested might even be Ottoman citizens? If that is the case, then the money they are seizing is Ottoman money! I shall send a letter to that troublesome pope in Europe, convincing him to free them immediately, lest he incur the wrath of the great and humble Sultan Suleiman."

Bowing her thanks, Gracia walked backward away from the throne to show her respect and left the sultan's palace. She hurried home to pen her own letter, as well.

"I will use all of my power to pull the prey away from this pope's teeth," Gracia said to Reyna. "I will remind him who he is crossing."

"Your Holiness, my most sincere congratulations on your recent appointment as pope," she wrote to Pope Paul. "Although we have never met, I send to you this generous gift of money to remind you of my longstanding friendship with the Vatican and with the many popes before you. And you can be assured that there will be more gifts to come in the future. In return, I ask only that you look in your heart and find the compassion to release my friends who languish in prison in Ancona."

The letter arrived at the Vatican and was brought to the pope's private office. It was placed on his desk next to the letter from Sultan Suleiman, the powerful leader of the Ottoman Empire.

But the pope's hate for Jews was deeper than his fear of the sultan. Deeper even than his love of Gracia's money.

Pope Paul looked at the letters lying on his desk, written to him by two of the most powerful people in the world. He lifted the papers up and crumpled them in his fist.

"Burn them," he said.

14

Revenge and Reunion

Istanbul, 1556–1560

In the year 1556, under the sweet skies of the Italian summer, twenty-four precious Jewish souls were burned at the stake in Ancona.

As the flames consumed these martyred Jews, their terrified wails filled the air. And far away, under the hot Turkish sun, Gracia's fury ignited.

"No more will we Jews be wood for their kindling!" she whispered, fiercely. "We will take revenge for the spilled blood of our brethren. Both the pope and the city of Ancona will suffer the consequences of what they have done."

"But what can you possibly do?" her new son-in-law, Joseph, asked. "How does one punish a pope? There is no man more powerful than him in all of Christendom."

"This pope is greedy, as all popes are," Gracia said, her eyes narrowing. "He has become fat and arrogant from the money he takes from the merchants around the world who unload their goods at the port of Ancona."

"Yes, this is true," Joseph said, confused. "But what has this to do with the death of our people?"

"I will use his greed to hurt him as he has hurt us," Gracia said. "We will boycott Ancona."

"Boycott Ancona?" Joseph asked, incredulous. "But that would require cooperation from all of the shipping agents across Europe and even in the Ottoman lands. All of the merchants, Jew and Gentile alike, would have to agree."

"Yes, that is exactly why you must travel back to Italy to speak with them," Gracia said, nodding. "You have always been very convincing."

"Of course," Joseph said, uncertainly. "I will pack my bags immediately and hope for the best."

"Don't just hope for the best, Joseph. Do your best," Gracia responded firmly. "I am counting on you. Tell the merchants that I am willing to pull out my own fleet from Ancona at great cost to my business. Meanwhile, I will arrange meetings with the prominent rabbis to get their support."

When Gracia met with the rabbis and told them of her plan, they were taken aback.

"My lady," the rabbis said, looking at her intently, "what you are proposing is very complicated. It will anger the pope and cause great financial loss to many people. We cannot agree to something like this lightly."

"Indeed, it will be difficult," Gracia agreed. "But this pope must be shown that Jewish blood is not cheap. He must pay for what he has done."

She pushed the papers across the desk to the rabbis. "I have written up this document, decreeing that no Jews should trade with Ancona," she said. "Will there be money lost? Perhaps. But how much is a Jewish life worth? How much are twenty-four Jewish lives worth? Please, I beg you, sign your names to this document."

The rabbis conferred for a few moments. Then the eldest among them spoke: "Doña Gracia," he said. "We have watched in awe and gratitude as you guided and supported our people. You have always worked to help the Jewish nation. We will honor your request."

For months, the ships withdrew from the port of Ancona. The local merchants watched in horror as the wharfs stood empty, and fewer and fewer ships docked to unload their merchandise.

From his seat in the Vatican, the pope read the plaintive letters from the merchants of Ancona. "Your Holiness, these Jewish refugees are a powerful force. In their anger, they have abandoned our port and we have suffered great losses."

Pope Paul seethed. His plan to harm the Jews had been matched by Gracia with a plan that harmed his people back. "I have been bested by a woman!" he shouted and flung his carafe of wine to the floor, watching the glass shatter and the ruby liquid spread across the tiles.

In the streets of Ancona, arrangements were made among the merchants to return some of the possessions of the arrested *conversos*. Slowly, the boycott ended, and life returned to normal.

While we did not manage to close down the port of Ancona forever, I am still very pleased with our effort, Gracia wrote in her diary. *Always, we Jews have been persecuted and hated by our enemies. And always, we have cried to them or bribed them or run away. But this time we fought back.*

Gracia looked down at the hand holding the pen. The elegant fingers were aging, the skin beginning to wrinkle. It was not the hand of the young girl who had written in her diary so many years before.

But the bracelet still glinted as brightly. She was still a link in the chain.

~

Back in Venice, where the cruel Inquisition still reigned, Brianda was growing uneasy.

"The hatred of this pope burns fiercely," she said to La Chica, "and I do not believe we are safe here anymore.

We must get your inheritance money back from the courts and then find a way to leave."

"But why would they let us leave?" asked La Chica.

"Don't worry, darling. If they will not let us leave, I have a plan that will make them force us to leave!"

"What is your plan, Mama?" La Chica asked.

"The law states that any *converso* will be banished from Venice," Brianda said. "And if they banish us, we could take our money and leave this wretched place."

"Marco!" Brianda called to her manservant. "Arrange a session with the council so that I may read a statement."

A week later, Brianda stood before the men of the court yet again.

"For many years I have been tormented here in Venice," she whimpered. "All that I want now is to live under Jewish law. In my heart, I have always been a Jew."

The council members were stunned. "Surely you cannot mean this! You yourself denounced your sister as a Jew. All of these years, you have sworn that you and your daughter live as sincere Christians!"

"It is my true will to live as a Jew," Brianda insisted, sniffing.

"Lady, you have tied our hands. You know that by law Jews can no longer stay in Venice!" the council answered. "Both you and your daughter are banished and must leave immediately!"

Brianda only smiled as she hurried to pack up her possessions and travel with La Chica back to Ferrara.

~

When the duke of Ferrara heard of Brianda's decision, he smiled.

"This is most excellent news," he told his squire. "The lady, Doña Gracia, will be so grateful to us for hosting her sister and niece that she will surely send us many gifts to show her gratitude."

He called for his scribe, to pen a letter to Gracia.

"How jubilant I feel as I welcome your sister and your niece once again! I fondly remember the days when you lived among us and shared your great generosity with my city," he wrote. "And now your family lives under my care! It is my honor to help you, my dear friend."

Duke Ercole is crafty, Gracia thought as she read the letter. *He writes this only in order to let me know that I owe him for this favor. But he is right. If he is hosting Brianda and La Chica, I am surely grateful to him.*

"Your Grace," Gracia responded, sending the letter along with a hefty gift of money. "Please accept this token of my appreciation for your friendship to our family."

Once Gracia had sent the letter, she breathed a deep sigh of relief. Finally, after all these years, Brianda and La Chica were safe.

"At least, I no longer have to worry that they are in Venice," she said to Reyna. "And perhaps, one day soon, Brianda's heart will soften and her anger will abate. I truly believe that we can be loving sisters again."

But it was not to be. Only a year after Brianda and La Chica settled in Ferrara, another letter arrived in Turkey. Gracia slit the wax seal and read.

"It is with eyes filled with tears that I write to you to inform you of Brianda's passing," Brianda's manservant had written. "She lived a difficult and confused life. Finally, her tormented soul can rest in peace."

"No!" Gracia whispered, her eyes filling with hot tears. "No!"

She tore her shirt and sank into a low chair in deep mourning. So many years wasted on a foolish feud! And now Brianda was gone, and they could never reconcile!

"My sister," she cried, "I always loved you. I hope that now, in the World of Truth, you can see this and understand it at last!"

When the seven days of mourning had passed, Gracia rose from her chair and sat at her desk. She rested her head in her hands and remembered the good times with Brianda. The jokes they had shared in their room together as girls. She remembered the long walks they took in Antwerp, and the times they spent cooking and laughing together.

This is how I will remember her from now on, Gracia thought.

As the happy, laughing sister that I loved. And I shall take care of La Chica as she would have wanted.

She lifted her head from her hands and wiped her eyes.

"Would you like to change out of your torn clothing, Mama?" Reyna asked.

"Before I do anything else, we must write a letter to Duke Ercole, convincing him to allow me to bring La Chica here to live with us," Gracia replied. "It is the only thing that I can still do for Brianda."

"Tell me what to say and I shall write it, Mama," Reyna said.

"Tell the duke of our family's great sadness. Appeal to his mercy, that surely a young orphaned girl must not be left alone in this cruel world. Request that I be made La Chica's guardian so she may be reunited with her only family."

Reyna nodded, "Yes, Mama."

When the duke's response arrived, Gracia read it quickly.

"Doña Gracia, I am so sorry for your loss," the duke wrote. "I too am in difficult circumstances. My treasury is low, and I would greatly benefit from a loan of your monies. Of course, I understand that you are the proper guardian for your niece. Do you think there is some way that we two could help each other now?"

Two can play at this game, thought Gracia. She quickly dashed off a response.

"Your Excellency, it is my honor to contribute to your treasury. In return, I ask only for your promise to allow the *conversos* to continue living safely in your land."

And what else could Duke Ercole do in the face of this powerful woman's determination? He agreed.

~

"Now that La Chica is under my guardianship, I must find her a worthy husband," Gracia said to Joseph.

Joseph cleared his throat. "I have been thinking of this as well. May I suggest my own brother, Samuel?" he said. "Although he has not been active in our family business, he is a good man and will be true to our heritage."

"That is a wonderful idea!" Reyna exclaimed. "If our husbands are brothers then La Chica and I would truly be sisters!"

"Yes!" Gracia said. "Let us send the news to La Chica along with a chest full of finery, lace for her wedding gown and jewels for her hair. We cannot travel to Ferrara for the wedding, but we can be there with her in thought and spirit."

It was a joyous celebration when La Chica married Samuel. Although Gracia and Reyna could not be there, they too danced and feasted in celebration of the young couple's marriage from their home in Istanbul.

After the wedding ceremony, the young couple traveled to join the family in Istanbul.

"Reunited!" Gracia breathed, her face shining. "My niece, we are together again, just as I promised."

Samuel and Joseph embraced warmly as La Chica cried tears of happiness into Gracia's shoulder. She stretched her arm out to include Reyna in her hug.

"Finally, we are all here where we belong, safe and happy at last!" Reyna said.

"Yes, safe and happy," Gracia said. "But still not where we belong."

15

The Promised Land

Istanbul, 1561

"This land has been good to us," Gracia said, drawing a deep breath. "We have prospered under Sultan Suleiman's rule. And yet … it is not our Promised Land."

"Promised Land, Mama?" Reyna said, furrowing her brow. "Are you referring to the land of the Jews promised to us in the Bible?"

Gracia nodded. "Yes, there in the Holy Land of our inheritance, I have found a city that I hope will be a place of refuge where the *conversos* escaping the Inquisition can finally find safety."

"A place for the refugees to live?" La Chica asked. "But what has that to do with us?"

Gracia gathered her thoughts and spoke slowly.

"For many years, I lived as a gentile, denying my true faith. I did not observe the holy Sabbath or the laws of kashrut. I kneeled in church. I swore in the name of a false god. Now, I am growing older and my past sits heavily upon my heart, but our sages say that he who walks four cubits within the Holy Land, all of his sins are forgiven."

"Mama!" Reyna said, putting her arm gently around Gracia's shoulder. "You did not sin! You were forced to live that way!"

"This is true," Gracia agreed, patting Reyna's hand. "And yet, it troubles me. And I find that my heart yearns to be in the city of Tiberias. To live as a Jew in the Jewish land."

"Why Tiberias?" asked Joseph.

"My sources say that it is an exceedingly beautiful place to live, with cool breezes coming off the waters, and hot springs to enjoy, plants and sugar cane and all of the riches of the seas."

"But is it not true that this area fell into ruin, abandoned after the Crusades? I am sure that there are many lovely places in the Holy Land," Joseph said. "Why not choose another town? Someplace already prospering?"

"There are certainly many beautiful places in the land," Gracia said, "but the great mystics write that those who are buried in Tiberias will be the first to be resurrected when the Messiah arrives. I have waited so very long to see the salvation of our people. I would like to be among the first to greet him when he finally comes."

The family were silent for a moment, thinking. Reyna spoke up first.

"Wherever you go, I will follow, Mama," she said, loyally.

"Of course," answered Joseph, coming up next to his wife.

"As will we," agreed La Chica and Samuel.

Gracia reached out to grasp their hands, "How fortunate I am to have such a loving family. You are all so good to me!"

"As you have always been good to us all, Mama," Reyna answered.

~

Gracia took a deep breath and uttered a short prayer asking for the wisdom to make her case before the sultan. Suleiman could well be angered by the thought of Gracia leaving his country and taking her money with her.

I must convince him that this idea is good for him as well. If the sultan approves my plan, I can make it happen. But if he does not … She shook her head. *I will do my best and pray for God's help*, she resolved.

"Your Magnificence, I have been made aware of a place in the Holy Land," Gracia said, "which is under Ottoman control. In this city, there are date palms and sugar cane and many areas suitable for the production of silk." She looked at the sultan's rich robe, "Silks such as those the sultan favors in his dress."

The sultan nodded. "Tell me more."

"Each year," Gracia continued, "thousands of Muslims, Christians and Jews gather in this place to enjoy the beautiful salt baths. The payment for these visits is given to the local Turkish deputy. Imagine, Your Magnificence, if so many people gather there when the place is ruined, how many more would come if the land were rebuilt? How much more money would they add to your treasury?"

The sultan stroked his smooth, trim beard, listening closely. "You may continue," he said.

"It is well known that you, the great sultan, the Wise One, have always aimed to spread security in all parts of your kingdom. Here is your chance to shine the light of your benevolent influence on this far corner of the world as well!"

The sultan smiled. "What is it that you propose, Doña Gracia?"

Gracia bowed her head humbly, "I, your most grateful servant, seek to rebuild this area of the land, with your kind permission. I dream that I may bring even greater honor to your throne."

"You have spoken well, my lady," the Sultan replied, flattered by her praise. "Not only will I allow you to build this community, but I will also give you money to begin the process."

Gracia hurried out of the palace, elated. There was much to be done before the work could begin. *But I have never been afraid of work. Certainly not when my dream is so close to becoming reality!*

~

"How are the plans for the new city coming along, Mama?" Reyna asked as they sat together in the parlor a few months later.

"Oh, Reyna." Gracia smiled. "Each day, I receive letters from my men, informing me of the city's progress. They are working hard to build houses and beautiful synagogues. There is even a Jewish school in which seventy scholars study our holy Torah!"

"So many people already?" Reyna asked.

"Yes! Here, read this letter I just received," Gracia said, handing her the paper. "Many Jews from Italy, Spain and Portugal are coming to settle there and finally live as Jews, just as I had hoped!"

"How wonderful!" Reyna responded. "When will we be ready to go?"

"I must finish wrapping up my business endeavors here in Turkey," Gracia said. "But I hope that we will be able to go as soon as next summer."

She turned from Reyna and brought her hand to her throat, suddenly overcome with emotion.

Here she sat in the parlor of her lovely home in Istanbul, a woman growing older. But as her mind's eye traveled, she saw herself touring the beautiful palace in Ferrara, gazing at the high buildings on the island city of Venice, looking for Diogo in the bustling port of Antwerp. She saw the maps on the wall above Francisco's desk. The innocent child brushing out her hair on the eve of her birthday and later trembling in the dark cellar of her childhood home.

"One day I will live freely as a Jew," that little girl had promised. "And everyone will know my name."

Gracia fingered the gold bracelet she had worn since the day she turned twelve. *I have tried so hard, Abuela,* she thought. *I have done my best to be a link in the chain.*

"Look, Mama," called Reyna, passing over the letter, "here at the bottom they write that they look forward with much anticipation to the arrival of 'the great and benevolent Lady, the proud Jewess who wears the crown of glory of Israel, Doña Gracia Benveniste Mendes Nasi.'" How flattering!"

Gracia ran her fingers gently over the words on the parchment. "They know my name," she said, softly.

"Whatever do you mean by that, Mama?" asked Reyna, confused.

"Oh, it is nothing, *querida,*" Gracia said, laughing lightly. "I am just remembering a promise that I made myself a long, long time ago."

Author's Note

Gracia Mendes Nasi was a woman of great power in a time when most women had no power. She was a person of faith, although she was forced to hide her faith. She was an activist and a dreamer and a businesswoman and a mother. She was one of the bravest women in Jewish history.

While this is a fictionalized account of Gracia's life, I have tried to give over her story faithfully, based on the historical evidence we have. Almost everything in this book is based loosely on the historical record, with a few exceptions. For instance, we do not actually have any evidence that Gracia kept a diary. I have written what I imagined a woman in Gracia's position might write in the privacy of her room. I imagined entries that show her hopes and dreams and fears, as a way of releasing those emotions from inside herself before she went out to face the world with the bravery and strength they had come to expect of her.

Gracia's niece, La Chica, was called Beatrice by the

family and only nicknamed La Chica in public documents. I used her nickname here to make it easier for the reader to differentiate between the two women.

Although Gracia yearned to settle in Tiberias, and actually built a thriving settlement there, she herself never made it to the Holy Land. Gracia died in Istanbul in the year 1569. Her loss was deeply felt throughout the Jewish world. Poets and scholars, rabbis and *conversos* mourned Gracia. In the words of Saadiah Lungo:

> Gone is the glitter,
> My morning is bitter,
> and broken my heart.

The State of Israel has honored Gracia with a commemorative medal and a museum in Tiberias devoted to her life. Both Philadelphia and New York City designated a day to be known as Doña Gracia Day. There have been festivals in her honor throughout Europe, with many historians calling her the Queen Esther of the Sixteenth Century. Gracia is remembered with love and reverence by the many hundreds of Jewish children born to the *conversos* she saved.

And she is remembered by us.

~

Author's Note

The poem quoted in Chapter 7 is from Samuel Usque's *Consolation for the Tribulations of Israel*, translated by Martin A. Cohen (Philadephia: Jewish Publication Society, 1965).

Nasi/Mendes Benveniste Family Tree

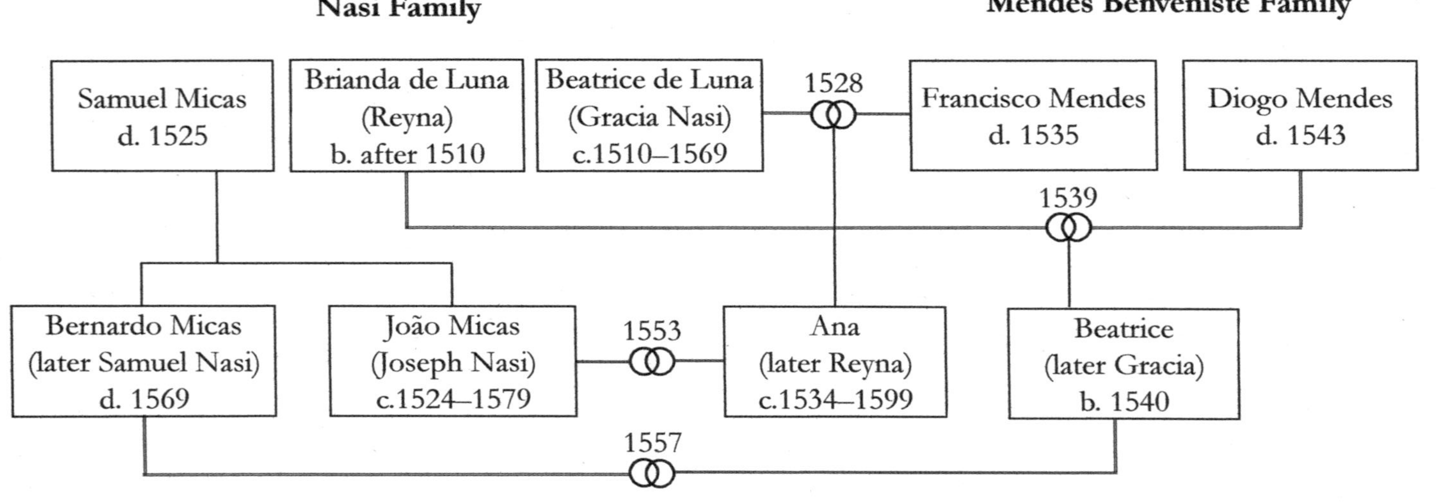

Timeline

1492 The Inquisition is announced in Spain
1510 Beatrice de Luna (Gracia) is born in Portugal
1528 Gracia marries Francisco Mendes
1536 Francisco dies. Gracia and Reyna travel to Antwerp, along with Brianda. The Inquisition is formally established in Portugal
1543 Diogo Mendes dies in Antwerp
1545 Gracia and Reyna escape to Venice
1550 Gracia and Reyna move to Ferrara. The Republic of Venice expels the *conversos*
1552 Plague breaks out in Ferrara
1553 The Ferrara Bible is published. Gracia and Reyna move to Istanbul
1556 Twenty-four Jews are burned to death. Gracia orders the boycott of the port of Ancona
1561 Gracia receives permission from Sultan Suleiman to begin a Jewish settlement in Tiberias
1569 Gracia dies in Istanbul